# Stepping up to Leadership

### ...the 21 steps to exceptional leadership

## Terry Lee

# Stepping up to Leadership

...the 21 steps to exceptional leadership

Terry Lee

Serenity Press books may be ordered through online booksellers or by contacting:

Serenity Press
www.serenitypress.org
serenitypress@hotmail.com

Because of the dynamic nature of the Internet, any web addresses or links contained in this book may have changed since publication and may no longer be valid. The views expressed in this work are solely those of the authors and do not necessarily reflect the views of the publisher and the publisher hereby disclaims any responsibility for them.

The author of this book does not dispense medical advice or prescribe the use of any technique as a form of treatment for physical, emotional, or medical problems without the advice of a physician, either directly or indirectly. The intent of the author(s) is only to offer information of a general nature to help you. In the event you use any of the information in this book for yourself, which is your constitutional right, the author(s) and the publisher assume no responsibility for your actions.

ISBN: (sc) 978-0-9925231-0-7
ISBN: (e) 978-0-9925231-1-4

# CONTENTS

# Acknowledgments

This book has grown out of the work I have done for over 20 years with many exceptional companies and their leaders at all levels. It is these leaders who time and again have demonstrated the truth that great leaders build great cultures, and without a great culture no strategy can be truly successful in creating a pathway to the vision. I would like to acknowledge the leaders in these companies who have allowed me to partner with them in building authentic leaders and strong leadership cultures. I have seen companies transformed and leaders who have stepped up to the challenge of leadership in companies such as Cisco Systems, CSL, Fuji Xerox, Bunnings, Officeworks, Honda, ANZ Bank, Clayton Utz Lawyers, Wesfarmers.

I have also learned a great deal from the colleagues I have been fortunate enough to work with at Mt. Eliza Business School in Australia, Ashridge Management College in the U.K., Center for Creative Leadership in the U.S. and Leadership Psychology in China.

My special thanks to Barbara for her never ending support, encouragement and love.

# Foreword

Leaders make the complex simple and the simple compelling.

Never has there been a better time to be a leader and never have our expectations of leaders been so great. Times of challenge and times of change call for leadership. If the world doesn't change then management is sufficient. However if the future is different or uncertain then only leadership will provide the solution. The more change required then the more leadership required.

In a world of complexity, uncertainty and rapid change no one person, no matter how talented a leader will have all the answers and provide all the energy required to drive this change. We need many leaders at many levels to provide the power and energy to transform organisations. Organisations don't transform when one person at the top sees things differently, they transform one by one when all people concerned begin to change how they see the world. No longer is one great leader no matter how charismatic capable of leading the change required. We need leadership in our organisations and in our communities that is widely dispersed, deeply embedded and driven by leaders who are building greater leadership capability in the people and teams they lead.

There has never been a better time to be a leader because never before has there been a greater opportunity for people to step up, and step forward as leaders. We are no longer looking for passive participants in our organisations and institutions. Rather we are looking for, and desperately need, active contributors who want to create the future.

This book is designed to help people who want to step up to leadership. All of us have a greater capacity to show leadership, all of us are needed to step forward to meet the challenges ahead. This book outlines a framework of 21 steps in 3 phases which will shape the leadership journey. The first phase and the foundational challenge of leadership is personal leadership. We don't need anyone's permission to be a better leader. We can all choose the leader that we want to be in our lives and in our work. There are 7 steps outlined that lead the way to effective personal leadership. That is, being the leader that you truly want to be, or need to be, in your life and in your work.

For some people personal leadership is sufficient, and all that is required in the way they lead their lives. If however you choose to lead others then a new responsibility emerges. That is a responsibility for the performance and development of others and for the teams in which they work. In many ways the only thing standing between an individual and the future is the leader they report to. Team leaders can keep people where they are or they can equip them for a greater future. The challenge of team leadership is the challenge of bringing out the best in people and teams and removing the impediments to their development. There are 7 steps outlined that lead the way to effective team leadership. That is, being the leader who truly and well serves the people who look to him/her for leadership.

After team leadership some people aspire, and are inspired, to lead and build long term successful organisations and institutions. This is the challenge of strategic leadership, which is concerned with taking organisations to the future and with sustainable success. This is the leadership required in the midst of extreme uncertainty and complexity to change mindsets and in collaboration with a diverse collection of stakeholders to transform relationships and the organisations within which we work. There are 7 steps outlined that contribute to effective strategic leadership. That is the inspiration and foresight to build the organisations of the future in a form that will have a beneficial impact on the way we live, and work together as people.

It seems to me that as leaders we have 3 levels of opportunity and responsibility:

1. Personal – to make the choice to be the best leader that we can be.
2. Team - to be the best at developing the people and building the teams.

3. Strategic – to contribute to the longer term success and sustainability of the organisations and communities within which we work and live.

This book is intended to help with these 3 challenges. The steps are not necessarily sequential, but eventually all 21 steps are necessary. Where you start depends on the need and your personal motivation, and whilst the steps do not have to be taken in order the 3 phases build one upon the other. Personal leadership, whilst it can be an end in itself, is a foundation for team leadership. You can't really be an effective team leader if you cannot lead yourself. Similarly you can't be an effective strategic leader if you cannot build teams. Managing your impact on others and building great teams is a necessary precursor to building enduring institutions.

Where you start is up to you, where you end up is dependent on how well you step up to the challenges of leadership on your journey.

# Introduction

Leadership is changing at a fast pace. Our expectations of leaders have grown sharply, our ideas about what constitutes effective leadership have changed significantly and our frustrations at a lack of leadership are mounting all of the time. Yet the concern for many is that confidence in our ability to develop leaders quickly enough and in sufficient quantities has not grown at the required pace. The context for the development of leadership has also changed. Where once it was seen as the responsibility of the organisation, today it is largely regarded as the responsibility of the individual, and ideally some combination of the two will be most effective in building broad and deep leadership capability.

Leadership is a very personal attribute. Clearly when it comes to executing a particular strategy or building a specific culture then the organisation will have a role to play, but by and large leadership today is a partnership between the individual and the group. A partnership between what I want to achieve as an individual and what the organisation needs to deliver for its diverse stakeholders. Today we look for alignment between what the individual stands for, and what the organisation needs.

Finding the right place to work, and to lead, is more critical to leadership than ever before. This is because so much is expected of leaders – they must be passionate, inspired, be honest in their dealings, responsible in their decisions and at the same time deliver the results expected. Today leaders are called on to give a great deal more of themselves. No longer is leadership just a role or a job. Today it is a calling, a sense of purpose, an important part of one's identity. Choosing the leader that one wants to be is an important life decision, understanding the leader the people need in a particular organisation, at a particular time, is an important strategic challenge.

Leaders today can also achieve more than ever before. Leaders can make a real difference to the organisations they lead, and to the communities they serve. The rate of change, the

Terry Lee

increased complexity of markets, the greater ambiguity in organisational life all mean that new ideas are called for and that new things are possible. It is expected today that leaders be change agents and catalysts for change and so it is accepted that they will act and not just accept the status quo. The speed of change today calls for leaders who are pro-active and not simply reactive.

Leaders are ultimately judged less by what they do and more by what they cause others to do. So whilst it is important for the leader to know what he/she stands for, this is ultimately futile if the leader cannot motivate and influence others to act. In the final analysis leadership is about the impact that the leader has, and this means that personal leadership must be seen within the strategic context of the time.

This book is written to help you to become an exceptional leader. The steps outlined will help you to better understand what leadership is, how it has changed and what it will mean in the future. On this basis the book's ultimate aim is to help you to become a better leader by increasing your ability to have an impact on the people that you lead now and the people you will lead in the future. This is one of the critical challenges of this, and every century, because the world, our communities and our organisations need all the leaders that we can get to take us from where we are today to where we could be tomorrow. In a very real sense it is the leadership that we get today that will determine the future we have tomorrow.

Leadership is not just learned by experience. Many people stuck in a rut repeat the same experience every day. This is not learning it is simply reinforcing habits. Leadership is learned by reflecting upon one's experience. The development of leadership is a thoughtful process, and is accelerated when the leader has a commitment to learning and to change and to creating the future. It is not just for those who are the brightest, nor for the most intuitive. It is for those with the three sights – hindsight, foresight and insight.

This is the hindsight to put history into perspective, to extract the learnings and not repeat the mistakes. The foresight to be able to anticipate what will happen and to build a vision which will be a driving force for action. Then the insight to understand why things happen and to make the right choices. Leadership is an interaction between cognitive intelligence and emotional intelligence – it is about being both bright and astute.

Leadership is at once both complex and simple. It is simple in concept, complex in context. Before we begin to look at it in greater detail however, there are some common myths that we need to explore. These myths have been embedded in conventional wisdom for some time, and they have restricted our ability to develop leaders and build leadership capability to the extent needed to deal with the challenges we face today.

**Myths about Leadership**

1. Leaders are born.

    There is no evidence that leaders are born and that leadership is a fundamentally inherited attribute. It is more likely that leadership is a contextual attribute and learned through experience. In this way the times make the leader and that it is the challenges faced through life that progressively build leadership style and capability. It is certain that we all bring into the world a set of attributes and potentials, but it is how the environment shapes them that determines the leader.

    *Leadership is less about talent and more about discipline and purpose.*

2. Leadership can't be learned.

    We know for certain that there are leadership skills and competencies that can be developed and improved. These are things such as the ability to give feedback, to provide recognition, to coach, to articulate a well-crafted vision. All of these can improve through life experience, through coaching, through training and through specific practice. These all can be improved but the desire to do so must be present as a pre-condition. Leadership is a collection of attributes, skills and values deployed in a specific context to achieve a particular result.

*Leadership is developed through life-long learning, adaptability and change.*

3. Leaders are extraverts.

   Extraverts may be more outgoing, more talkative, and more sociable, but there is no evidence that they make better leaders. Introverts bring their own style and preferences to leadership and can be just as effective in achieving outcomes. Leaders who are introverted tend to be more reflective, less impulsive and to be better listeners and there are times when these are exactly what is required of leaders. Today the effective leader needs to do both at the right time and in the right way.

   *Leaders need a range of approaches for different situations.*

4. Leaders must be in control.

   Traditionally leaders were seen as bosses, as someone taking charge, as someone who wanted control. At its extreme leaders were "control freaks" who were prone to micro-manage.  The reality today is that it is micro-management that people resent and react poorly to and it is the style that empowering organisations are determined to remove. People with a strong need for control are more likely to create dependency and a passive workforce rather than the empowered, self-directed and innovative workforce we seek today.

   *Leadership is inspiring and bringing out the best in the people you lead.*

5. Leadership comes with the job.

   This is the most dangerous myth of all.  The idea that people in a leadership role will necessarily display leadership. It is essential today that all those in leadership roles display leadership, but the sad reality is that many still don't.  We still have far too many leaders who are really managers of process and task, rather that leaders of people and purpose.

***Leaders don't take leadership from the team, they build it in.***

6. Leadership is only required at work.

The reality is that leadership is something that we bring to our life. The essential question is: are you leading your life, or is your life leading you. Leadership is an attribute of the person and it is a quality that we bring to the whole of our life. It is how we lead our lives and what we choose to do with our lives that determines our life satisfaction. Leadership starts with the personal and then in organisations moves to the team and the strategic. It starts with self-awareness and is then sustained through self-management

***Leadership is bringing more of who you truly are to the way you choose to lead.***

7. Leadership is for the few.

In any organisation or team if only a few are stepping up to leadership then the team will never fulfil its potential. It doesn't require all to lead, all of the time, but a high performance team is built on the active contribution of all members to team process and team outcomes. The greatest growth opportunity for all organisations today is to unlock the so far unrealised potential of its people and teams. It is through active participation and the right contribution that talent is tapped and potential is unlocked. It requires people who know when to lead and when to follow and people who are passionate about bringing out the best in themselves and their teams.

***Leadership is a human capability necessary for organisational and team success.***

In the final analysis leadership is a personal challenge, an organisational challenge and ultimately a challenge facing the communities in which we all live. In times of rapid change there is a need for greater leadership than ever. Leadership is required to take us through uncertainty and to give us the future than we need and that we dream of. Today more then ever before we are looking for leadership at the personal, team and organisational levels.

Leaders who step up are those who master the 21 steps on the leadership journey. These steps are grouped into three broad phases – personal, team and strategic.

## Personal Leadership

1. Leaders are self-aware
2. Leaders have a clear vision
3. Leaders are skilled communicators
4. Leaders live their values
5. Leaders manage their impact
6. Leaders seek new ideas
7. Leaders are resilient

## Team Leadership

8. Leaders attract the right people
9. Leaders get the best out of people
10. Leaders build shared understanding
11. Leaders give recognition to others
12. Leaders address performance issues
13. Leaders inspire people
14. Leaders help teams to succeed

## Strategic Leadership

15. Leaders develop shared vision
16. Leaders build performance cultures
17. Leaders change mindsets
18. Leaders unlock the hidden value in people and teams
19. Leaders embrace learning and drive change
20. Leaders set a positive example
21. Leaders have a clear strategic agenda

**The key message**

It is a great time to be a leader, a great time to show true leadership.

There are three important questions at the start of our leadership journey:

1. What type of leader will you strive to be?
2. How will you judge your success as a leader?
3. What type of leadership will the times require and do the people need?

This book is intended to help you to find the answers to these questions and to then offer a framework for your own personal leadership development.

**Where do you start?**

You can start where your behaviour is strongest and your capabilities clearest, or start where the need is greatest and the greatest challenge lies. In a developmental sense you can take the time to build a comprehensive array of strengths. If we are all a work in progress on the leadership journey, then this is indeed a life long journey.

If on the other hand you start with the current context, then it might be best to start where there is the greatest demand. Wherever you start and whenever you start, you should understand the current strategic context and identify the challenges you, your team and the organisation face. You can then begin to see the steps that are critical to success, and with this in mind put in place a clear plan of action.

This book is intended to help you to understand the challenge involved in exceptional leadership, and then to give you some practical exercises as a starting point. Working with a trusted friend or mentor can accelerate the process. If you decide to master the 21 steps you will have made a significant investment in the development of exceptional leadership capability. If you are interested in improving your leadership at a personal level the first seven steps should be your focus. Effectively leading a team takes in the first fourteen steps. Strategic leadership at an organisational level extends to the full twenty one steps.

So let's begin.

# Part one

# Personal Leadership

The start is to decide that you want to be a leader and make the decision to show leadership in your own life. This is the decision that you don't simply want to follow the lead of others or to be at the mercy of circumstance. There are times of course when you need to be a follower, and in fact want to be a follower. The astute person knows when to lead and when to follow.

Personal leadership means deciding to take charge of your own life and create your own destiny. It means setting a direction, using your initiative and focusing on the results you want to achieve. It means being positive, looking for opportunities and taking responsibility for your own actions. It means being accountable and not just promising something to keep others happy. Personal leadership means bringing more of who you truly are to the way you choose to lead.

**There are seven steps to master:**

1.   Leaders are self-aware – understand yourself   and what is important to you

2.   Leaders have a clear vision – be clear about where you want to go or what you want to achieve

3.   Leaders are skilled communicators – be good at listening and talking to others

4.   Leaders live their values – display behaviour that is consistent with your values

5.   Leaders manage their impact – be aware that leadership is less what you do and more what you cause others to do

6.    Leaders seek new ideas – keep an open mind and continually look for  better ways to do things

7.    Leaders are resilient – be able to bounce back from adversity

The starting point for the leadership journey is personal leadership. Once this is established you then have a solid foundation for building team leadership, which is the ability to build high performance teams and to influence and develop others. Then comes strategic leadership which is the leadership required to align vision, strategy and culture in order to build a successful and sustainable organisation.

# Step one:

# Leaders are self-aware

Leading yourself is the step before leading others and the starting point for this is knowing yourself. A good way to increase self-awareness is to put aside some time on a regular basis to reflect upon your vision, your strengths and weaknesses, and importantly your impact on the mood, motivation and confidence of the people you lead.. Understanding yourself is the basis of all further development. Understanding what is important to you, helps you to understand what is not important to you and this helps you to clarify what it is that you really want to do. Finding the thing you love makes it easy to be passionate about leading.

## What this step means

The best leaders know themselves well. They are aware of their thoughts and moods and recognise how these affect their thinking and also influence the decisions they make. They also are aware of the impact their mood has on the mood, motivation and confidence of others. The foundation of leadership is self awareness and the discipline of leadership is self management. The ability to self-manage is dependent upon the level of awareness of the leader, because you can't manage something that you are not aware of.

When leaders are clear what they stand for, they can then be clear about what they don't stand for. They can then be more certain about their priorities and understand what they are prepared to do and what they are not prepared to do. Leaders need to reflect upon their values and aspirations and about the type of leader they are trying to be. When making decisions in complex situations it is helpful to know what is negotiable and what is non-negotiable. Leaders need to know this from an organisational and strategic perspective, but equally from a personal one.

## How this step has changed

In the past there was little expectation that managers would be self-aware. It would not have been part of the job description. It was not regarded as an important part of a manager's role at a time when management was concerned primarily with direction, compliance and control. With the rise to importance of leadership, self awareness became an important part of a leader's style because leadership is concerned with the capacity to influence and inspire. The more leaders were expected to influence and inspire the greater the focus on the nature of their impact and the greater the emphasis on having flexibility in style.

All of this requires leaders to have high self awareness of their style, their impact and their ability to change. This requires leaders to have insight into their feelings, their thinking and their patterns of behaviour. Self-awareness and a high level of emotional intelligence will be a critical attribute for any exceptional leader and will be increasingly so into the future. Experience and technical skill help you to know what to do, but it takes highly attuned emotional intelligence to know how to take people with you.

## What this step means for you

Self awareness is now regarded as the cornerstone of leadership and a critical foundation for current and future success. If you were judged to have low self awareness then this would be a severely limiting factor in any career. It would most likely be perceived that you are set in your ways and may be resistant to change. In a dynamic, rapidly changing world such a reputation would reduce the leadership opportunities that were offered. Leaders today receive vast amounts of feedback about their style – they receive it from bosses, from peers, and from direct reports. They will also receive it from customers and increasingly from investors and from communities in which they operate. It means that leaders must be comfortable to receive feedback, confident enough to ask for it, and have enough courage to accept it gracefully even when it is negative. It is important to accept that feedback will be a central part of any leader's life and to appreciate that it plays a major role in every leader's development.

## What you can do:

1.  Use the power of reflection

    Put aside time to reflect on what you want to achieve, what      you stand for and what you have done. We don't necessarily learn from doing, especially if we keep doing the same thing and responding in the same way. Learning comes from reflecting on our experience, evaluating it and making modifications for the future.

2. Ask for feedback

   Ask people who are important in your work and life for feedback. Ask your team for feedback about the impact of your behaviour and what you might do to be more effective. Ask people you respect for feedback on things that are more personal for you.

3. Clarify your values

   Picture your behaviour through the day and consider what message it might communicate to the people around you. Think about the values that are important to you and consider whether your behaviour is consistent with these values.

4. Learn from others

   Recall the leaders you have had and consider what aspects of their style you would adopt and what you wouldn't. What was it that the leaders who inspired you really did?

5. Give credit to those who have helped you

   Reflect upon the mentors and others in your life who have contributed to your development and consider the impact that they have had. What was it that they did which had a significant impact on your development? What is it that you are doing to contribute to develop others?

**A final reminder**

Self awareness is an on-going challenge. It is important to be aware of your thinking, your feelings and your mood in general. The best leaders are also aware of their behaviour at all times and are sensitive to the impact they are having on others. It will be easier to do this if you make it a priority to set aside time on a regular basis to reflect on what is happening in your life and what is important in your life and how closely aligned the two are.

Some people like to do this at the start of the day, and some prefer to reflect at the end of the day. Some combine it with a walk, whilst others prefer to find a quiet place to think. Whatever works best for you is the best thing to do. If you can build it into your daily or weekly routine it will be easier to make it a priority. Being in control of you is a critical part of leadership; understanding you is the starting point.

## Development plan for mastering this step: Self-awareness

### 1. What more do I need to know?

To take this step I need to know more about.....

### 2. What are the benefits of taking this step?

If I could master this step it would enable me to.....

### 3. What might make this hard to do?

The challenges I face in taking this step are.....

### 4. What would I have to change?

The behaviours I need to adopt to complete this step are.....

### 5. What might be some obstacles?

The things that might stop me from taking this step are.....

### 6.  Where do I start?

The first thing I need to do to get started is to.....

### 7. What would help me to succeed?

The supports I would need to put in place to help me to take this step are.....

### 8. What would be the signs of success?

I would know I had been successful in taking this step when.....

# Step two:

# Leaders have a clear vision

Once you know what is important to you, you then need to be clear about what it is that you want to achieve. Having a clear purpose makes it easy to be passionate about what you do and it is this passion which will inspire others and also give you the resilience to withstand the inevitable setbacks. Once you have a clear vision it makes decisions about priorities and pathways for development much easier. It is hard to make sound decisions in the absence of a clear direction.

## What this step means

Leaders must have a vision of where they want to go. If you are not taking people somewhere, you are by any definition not leading. Leadership is taking people from where they are today to the future. Being dissatisfied with the way things are and challenging the status quo are key characteristics of leadership. Finding a better way is a powerful drive for leaders. The vision does not have to be monumental it just has to be something better. It is a picture that the leader holds in his/her minds eye. It is a standard that is set that can be used to guide achievement. It is both a source of motivation and a source of satisfaction. It has elements that are both conceptual and emotional. The magnitude of the vision is the conceptual and appeals to the cognitive domain, whereas the worth of the vision connects emotionally.

## How has this step changed

If life doesn't change a great deal vision is not very important. If the future is likely to be more of the same then there is no need for vision, because what we see today is what we will see tomorrow. However, the more things change and the more uncertain things become, the more important it is to have a clear vision. Today leaders are challenged to have vision at the very time when greater complexity and uncertainty makes it difficult to foresee the future.

In large, dispersed organisations the vision is also used to ensure that everyone is heading in the same direction. It also is important when empowering people and pushing down decision making to provide the vision as a framework to ensure that the right decisions are made and the right priorities established. It is the vision which ultimately inspires people in their work and creates hope and the belief in people of what is possible for them, their teams and the organisation. Vision today is considered to be the staring point for not only strategy, but also for the development and engagement of the individual.

## What this step means for you

It is very difficult to develop as a leader without a vision of the type of leader you are trying to be and without a clear understanding of the impact you want to have.  The vision is your dream of your personal best as a leader.  It is a picture in your mind of the leader you would be proud to be.  The vision helps you to make important decisions today about what you are prepared to do now and about the trade-offs you are willing to make in order to become that leader.  It helps you to decide what you are prepared to do and just as important what you are not prepared to do.  The vision you have of yourself as a leader is also intimately connected with the vision you have of the future for whatever project or challenge you are working on.  Being able to visualise success is an important attribute of exceptional leaders

## What you can do:

1.  Develop your own leadership vision

    Write a statement of your own personal leadership vision. What is important to you as a leader?  What is the deeper purpose that drives your leadership?  What type of leader would you would like to be in five years.

2.  Identify development experiences

    Consider the capabilities you would need to build to achieve your leadership vision.  What experiences would you need to have over the next five years that would help you to build these capabilities?

3.  Establish short term priorities

    Future development starts with today.  What do I have to start doing and stop doing?  Consider the priorities you would need to set for the next twelve months to begin the process of further leadership development.

4. Look to your role models

   Talk to leaders you admire or work with to understand what drives them and what leadership means to them. Identify what they are good at and what impact this has on you.

5. Review past success

   Think about times in the past when you have been most successful as a leader. What were you most passionate about? Where did your real capabilities lie?

## A final reminder

Goals and objectives can direct your attention and motivate you but it is only through having a compelling vision that you will be inspired. A vision can inspire because it connects the goals to a deeper purpose. It is something that draws on emotion and not just logic. That is why vision is sometimes difficult to articulate, because it is more of an idea or a picture in the mind, rather than something that is neatly defined. It is important because whilst the logic gives the direction the emotional component sustains the passion. Vision brings focus and focus enables the leader to harness energy, and it is harnessing energy in the pursuit of a worthwhile goal that makes leadership so effective.

## Development plan for mastering this step: Having a Clear Vision

### 1. What more do I need to know?
To take this step I need to know more about.....

### 2. What are the benefits of taking this step?
If I could master this step it would enable me to.....

### 3. What might make this hard to do?
The challenges I face in taking this step are.....

### 4. What would I have to change?
The behaviours I need to adopt to complete this step are.....

### 5. What might be some obstacles?

The things that might stop me from taking this step are.....

### 6. Where do I start?

The first thing I need to do to get started is to.....

### 7. What would help me to succeed?

The supports I would need to put in place to help me to take this step are.....

### 8. What would be the signs of success?

I would know I had been successful in taking this step when.....

# Step three:

# Leaders are skilled communicators

In almost every organisation if you ask the people employed what needs to be done to improve effectiveness, they will say that communication needs to be improved. Of course communication means more than just the words that are spoken and the messages delivered. Communication includes the information that is shared, the feedback that is given and the extent to which people feel involved in the decisions that are made.

The nature of communication reflects the level of transparency that exists, and the extent to which people are open to, and open with, others. Communication is non verbal as well as verbal. From the leader's perspective it is true that actions speak louder than words, and so what you stand for as well as how you express it and how you engage others are all powerful forms of communication. Communication is primarily about connecting. Its effectiveness is determined by its impact.

## What this step means

Leaders have to be excellent communicators in order to engage the people that they lead. They need to communicate in order to create understanding and to ensure that objectives and priorities are aligned across their teams. But exceptional leaders also know that communication goes two ways and it is the ability to actively listen as well as to effectively articulate that is most powerful. Vision cannot be shared without the ability to engage others, and performance cannot be improved without the ability to give direct, yet supportive, feedback. The most important reason why communication is critical is that leaders cannot unleash the potential of the people they lead if they do not know them well, if they cannot communicate in a genuine and personal way, and if they cannot inspire them with what is possible.

## How this step has changed

We have moved a long way from the boss at the top of the organisation giving instructions without recourse to the opinions or contributions of others. Organisations rely on multiple strategies for effective communication today. They communicate what they stand for through their brand to their customers. They communicate their sense of corporate responsibility to their investors and the communities they serve. They communicate to their own people in a myriad of ways through the environment they create to the announcements and policies they distribute. A comprehensive communication strategy is designed to appeal to the heart as well as to the head.

However we know that the most powerful way in which leaders communicate, and the one that has the greatest impact on culture and performance, is the personal example set by leaders themselves. It influences the thinking of their people and also influences their adoption of certain behaviours. When the leader's behaviour aligns with what the leader says it sends a message which reinforces the integrity and trustworthiness of the leader.

## What this step means for you

Leaders have to become skilled in the art and science of communication. It means thinking through not only what you want to say but also want people need to hear. A leader needs to be sensitive to whether people are looking for encouragement or for challenge or whether they need direction or support. Leaders need to deliberately practice their communication skills whether they are talking to large groups, to small teams or to an individual. They need to be skilled at crafting a message and also at delivering it. They do not need to do these things alone. Most astute leaders understand when they need support and assistance and when the message is better delivered by someone else. Leaders need to practice when to speak and when to be quiet, when to be actively involved and when to just listen. In order to do this they need high levels of self awareness and high levels of self discipline. The best will have a range of mentors and a network of supporters who will give them regular feedback.

## What you can do

1. Be clear about the purpose of the communication

   Take the time to think about the real purpose of any communication. Be clear about what you want to achieve and what the key messages are. You don't have to say everything, just sufficient to create understanding and have the impact you want.

2. Learn from the masters

   Watch people closely who are good communicators. Watch what they do and study the impact they have. Decide if there are things they do that you might want to adopt and things they do that you would not want to adopt.

3. Reflect upon the impact of communication on you

Be aware of the impact of communication on you so that you can be sensitive to the emotional impact of a message and how it is delivered. How does the message and how it is delivered make you feel? What emotion does it evoke?

4. Welcome opportunities to communicate

Don't take lightly the opportunity to communicate. When people listen to you they are giving you their time and attention so use it wisely. Treat every opportunity with respect and seek to learn and to improve every time.

5. See you as others see you

Record yourself giving a speech or presentation. Set aside time to watch the replay to see yourself in action and look for opportunities for improvement.

**A final reminder**

Communication is something that we all need to work on all of the time. Whenever surveys are done looking at organisational improvement one solution that is almost always proposed is "better communication". Learning how to express your ideas more clearly and with greater impact, and learning how to listen more effectively, are key leadership skills to master. Knowing when to talk and when to listen is the sign of an astute leader. Consider the impact you wish to have and tailor your communication content and process accordingly.

## Development plan for mastering this step: Being a Skilled Communicator

**1. What more do I need to know?**

To take this step I need to know more about.....

**2. What are the benefits of taking this step?**

If I could master this step it would enable me to.....

**3. What might make this hard to do?**

The challenges I face in taking this step are.....

**4. What would I have to change?**

The behaviours I need to adopt to complete this step are.....

### 5. What might be some obstacles?

The things that might stop me from taking this step are.....

### 6. Where do I start?

The first thing I need to do to get started is.....

### 7. What would help me to succeed?

The supports I would need to put into place to help me take this step are.....

### 8. What would be the signs of success?

I would know I had been successful in taking this step when.....

# Step four:

# Leaders live their values

We all have values and we all show what our values really are through our behaviour. It doesn't matter what we think our values are, people watch what we do and then make a judgement about what our values really are. Leaders because they step forward to lead, and because of the impact they have upon the people they lead, have a high profile. People closely watch what they do and then make judgements about them. It is critical therefore for leaders to be clear about what they stand for and equally what they don't stand for. Leaders because they are always on display need the discipline to practice what they preach because this forms the basis of perceptions of integrity – and for a leader integrity is everything.

**What this step means**

Leaders must live the values that they espouse. People look for consistency between what they say and what they do. Leaders are important role models for the culture and so their behaviour must model the values they are trying to promote. In this way they must be careful about what they espouse and promote because this is the standard they will be held to. When there is a perceived gap between what leaders say and what they do this undermines their credibility and increases cynicism. Cynicism then drives out learning and undermines performance. Leaders build trust by following through on commitments and making sure there is close alignment between their words and actions. If leaders are not trusted then there is nothing for them to build upon and no matter what else they do it will not be effective.

**How this step has changed**

There is clear evidence that the culture that develops in any organisation is a direct consequence of what the leaders do. In other words it is their behaviour and priorities that drives culture. We also know that the culture is a physical manifestation of the values observed. It doesn't matter what people say their values are, the reality is that they are expressed in the behaviours exhibited. It is important therefore for leaders to be clear about the values that they want to see embedded in the culture and to then have the discipline to behave according to these values themselves.

The expectation today is that leaders will lead in a way that is conducive to the culture that the organisation is trying to build and that they will do this consistently and genuinely. In this way culture originates in the senior leadership team and is then consolidated by the way that the leaders at all levels, and in all teams, practice and reinforce the agreed behaviours.

**What this step means for you**

It means that you have to be clear about your values and priorities as a leader. Be clear about what you stand for and clear about what you don't stand for. This is the only way that you will know what organisation or team to work with. If you are to promote through your actions the values of an organisation then you need to be clear about what they are so you know if they align with your own values. You cannot genuinely espouse values that are not aligned with your own values. You can try but you will never do it well and you will never do it with passion or with integrity. It means that finding what work you want to do, and finding who you want to work with, are an important challenge in life and a key part of becoming an effective leader.

**What you can do:**

1.  Make a list of your core values

    Consider the values that are most important to you personally. Make a list and check the ones that you would like to think are a key part of your leadership style.

2.  Describe behaviours that demonstrate the values

    Describe the behaviours which would best express these values in a range of situations. Assess how well your behaviours reflect these. What is the gap between what you want and what people see?

3.  Seek evidence that confirms

    Look for evidence (eg. feedback) that supports the alignment between your values and your behaviour. Ask people to give you feedback.

4.  Conduct a time analysis

    Identify the key priorities that you have as a leader and assess the amount of time you devote to each. Do you spend time doing the things that are most important to you or are you neglecting key priorities in your life and work?

5.  Discuss with a trusted advisor

    Have a talk with a mentor about values and the challenge of bringing your values more fully to the way you lead. Talking with a trusted advisor, especially one who challenges you, is a good way to bring clarity to complex issues.

## A final reminder

Being clear about your values makes it easier for you to understand what you really stand for, and this makes it easier to decide what work you really want to do, and also who you really want to work with. This makes it easy for you to lead in a way that is consistent with your values. Doing something you don't want to do, with people you don't really like, means that you have to motivate yourself constantly just to perform. Over time this is more likely to produce cynicism in others and long term dissatisfaction in yourself. Being genuine as a leader mans being the leader you truly want to be.

## Development plan for mastering this step: Living my Values

### 1. What more do I need to know?

To take this step I need to know more about.....

### 2. What are the benefits of taking this step?

If I could master this step it would enable me to.....

### 3. What might make this hard to do?

The challenges I face in taking this step are.....

### 4. What would I have to change?

The behaviours I need to adopt to complete this step are.....

### 5. What might be some obstacles?

The things that might stop me from taking this step are.....

### 6. Where do I start?

The first thing I need to do to get started is to.....

### 7. What would help me to succeed?

The supports I would need to put in place to help me to take this step are.....

### 8. What would be the signs of success?

I would know I had been successful in taking this step when.....

# Step five:

# Leaders manage their impact

Effective leadership does not happen by accident, it occurs by design. The best leaders start with the results in mind and determine the best strategy for achieving those results. It means leaders don't just do what they want to do; they do what the situation demands of them. It is not about the leader, it is about the people being led. This means leaders need to be in tune with the context and with the mindsets of the people being led. They then need to determine the behaviour or approach which will have the desired effect.

## What this step means

The best leaders spend a lot of time thinking about the impact they want to have. They understand the simple truth that it is less what the leader does and more what the leader causes others to do that is important. The single most important person for any worker is the person they report to. This person creates the context, clarifies the expectations and provides the recognition or lack of it. Being treated with respect by the leader is a powerful motivating force for each person and has a significant compound impact on each individual's self esteem. When leaders build the self esteem of the people they lead, they also begin the process of building their confidence to achieve.

## How this step has changed

We are aware today that what leaders do, for good or bad, has an impact. No longer can leaders do whatever they want to do, now it is expected that leaders will behave according to the values and principles of the organisation concerned and will act in ways that ensure its long term strategic success. Leaders today therefore need a good deal more self discipline than would have been required or expected in the past and they need a good deal more self awareness so that they can monitor their impact.

It is easy in organisations to see the impact of leaders throughout their careers. Good leaders build teams and poor leaders undermine them. Good leaders attract and retain talented people, poor leaders lose them. Good leaders get results over time, poor leaders can often get good results in the short term, and can often derive the benefits of an existing positive culture, but cannot sustain results over time.

## What this step means for you

It means that as a leader you have to be alert to, and sensitive to, your impact upon others. It means that you need ways to get feedback about your behaviour and you need to have people who will be candid and open with you. It also means that as a leader you have to have flexibility in your approach and possess a range of styles that you can deploy as a leader. The day is long gone when as a leader you can have just one style in all situations. Whilst it is true that leaders need to be consistent they also need to be adaptable and flexible in their approach. Consistency needs to be in principles, values and ethics but flexibility is in the way that they are expressed.

Leaders need to keep an open mind, learn from others and ensure that their behaviour is driven by their strategic objectives and not just their own personal preferences.

**What you can do:**

1.  Review your own behaviour

    Reflect upon how much flexibility you have in the way you behave and how much care you take with how you behave. Consider how much your behaviour is driven by your vision and your long term objectives, rather than just your immediate needs.

2.  Look at your options

    Think about the impact you have on others and the results you are seeking to achieve. Consider the range of options you have in any situation? How often do you access a range of options rather than fall back upon a habitual response.

3.  Think about your criteria for success

    Consider how you judge your effectiveness as a leader. What would be your criteria for success as a leader? In other words what would I need to do, or achieve, to consider myself a success as a leader?

4. Seek feedback

   Ask for feedback about your impact from people who you have an important relationship with. Show a genuine interest in learning and ask how you could provide greater support or modify your approach.

5. Review the impact of mood on behaviour

   Review how much your mood, rather than your values, drives your behaviour from day to day. Is it how you feel at any time that determines how you act, rather than your core values or what is important to you?

**A final reminder**

You come to lead not because you have nothing better to do but because you want to have an impact and to make a difference. That difference you can make and what you can achieve will always be greater when it is done through others. Leadership is a professional as well as a personal responsibility because it requires a high level of self discipline and self management. When you are leading it is not being self focused it is about being results focused. The best leaders think before they act, they monitor their impact, and then modify their behaviour.

## Development plan for mastering this step: Managing my Impact

### 1. What more do I need to know?

To take this step I need to know more about.....

### 2. What are the benefits of taking this step?

If I could master this step it would enable me to.....

### 3. What might make this hard to do?

The challenges I face in taking this step are.....

### 4. What would I have to change?

The behaviours I need to adopt to complete this step are.....

### 5. What might be some obstacles?

The things that might stop me from taking this step are.....

### 6. Where do I start?

The first thing I need to do to get started is to.....

### 7. What would help me to succeed?

The supports I would need to put in place to help me to take this step are.....

### 8. What would be the signs of success?

I would know I had been successful in taking this step when.....

# Step six:

# Leaders seek new ideas

Leaders can't stand still. They need to be ahead of what is happening, focussed on the vision and making decisions today which will move the organisation, the team or the individual forward. They need confidence, but at the same time the humility, to know that whilst accountability might ultimately rest with them, they can never be the only one with ideas. Leadership is a constant challenge to understand what is happening and to find a better way to do things. Leaders appreciate that new ideas don't always come from outside, sometimes the best come from tapping the collective imagination and intelligence of the team.

## What this step means

Leaders bring in new ideas. They are drivers of innovation. They are open with others, but it is their openness to others, that is the core of innovation. They seek new ideas and possibilities and whilst they won't necessarily accept everything they hear it is their openness that stimulates innovation. When leaders listen and ask for input and then consider suggestions they receive, it encourages others to offer more and better ideas. When leaders have fixed views or are difficult to influence the people give up and stop making suggestions. It is the capacity to influence that gives people a reason to persist. When leaders are able to be influenced, people will give them more ideas and this enables them to make better decisions. This process also ensures greater ownership of the decisions taken

## How this step has changed

It is essential that leaders have a strategic mindset and understand the environment in which they operate. It is also essential that they have a culture mindset and are sensitive to the internal factors that drive human thinking and behaviour. Leaders have to work "on the team" and keep their teams open to new ways of thinking. They also need to ensure that teams keep a strategic mindset and operate within the context of the changing external environment. Building performance and trust in a team is only a first step, having those teams then manage the stakeholders in the external environment takes the team to the next level. Finding ways to stimulate and challenge teams and individuals and giving them the motivation to change is a leadership challenge. Leaders cannot do this well if they do not first embrace and model innovation themselves.

## What this step means for you

It means that you have to have a strong determination to find a better way in everything that you do. It means that you will need a plan for leadership development which will outline how you will find new ways of doing things. It means that you will need a range of sources to challenge your thinking and give you new ideas or information. These can be on-line resources or print resources or people or network associations. Leaders must read widely or at least think widely in order to identify emerging trends in the environment. The best leaders look for people with different perspectives. They look for people who are curious and see things that others miss.

**What you can do:**

1. Keeping informed

   Reflect upon your major sources of information or ideas? How diverse, widespread or credible are they? Where do your new ideas come from and how do you keep stimulating your thinking?

2. Attend conferences, meetings and associations

   Review the conferences or meetings that you attend. How selective and strategic are you and to what extent are you constantly looking to find new avenues for learning? How much do the ones you currently attend challenge your thinking and give you new perspectives?

3. Seek ideas from the team

   Hold a regular meeting with your team or set up a workgroup to brainstorm new ideas. Invite different people to attend to hear from new contributors and to bring different voices into the conversation.

4. Take a class

   Enrol in a creative thinking class or join a practical philosophy group.

5.  Review meeting time

    Estimate how much time is spent in your discussions
    with others searching for new ideas and challenging
    conventional wisdom. How much time is devoted to the
    status quo and business as usual?

## A final reminder

Leadership is about the future and about change.  It is not
about heading backwards and so of necessity it involves the
unknown.  Therefore you need to be open to new ideas and
you need to access new ideas to stimulate your thinking and
to challenge conventional wisdom.  The best in any field stay
at the top of their game because they continually innovate.
Resting on your laurels can bring short term success, but it
is the relentless drive to improve, to simplify and to adapt
which sustains success.  It is an asset to be curious about
the world and to be interested in how things work. In a
world of discontinuous change where no one can with
confidence predict the future, nothing can be discounted.

Terry Lee

## Development plan for mastering this step: Seeking New Ideas

**1. What more do I need to know?**
To take this step I need to know more about.....

**2. What are the benefits of taking this step?**
If I could master this step it would enable me to.....

**3. What might make this hard to do?**
The challenges I face in taking this step are.....

**4. What would I have to change?**
The behaviours I need to adopt to complete this step are.....

### 5. What might be some obstacles?

The things that might stop me from taking this step are.....

### 6. Where do I start?

The first thing I need to do to get started is to.....

### 7. What would help me to succeed?

The supports I would need to put in place to help me to take this step are.....

### 8. What would be the signs of success?

I would know I had been successful in taking this step when.....

# Step seven:

# Leaders are resilient

As the world gets more complex and as the challenges come faster leaders need to have the stamina to stay the course. They need to respond quickly to inevitable setbacks and pick themselves up when things don't go according to plan. They need to be able to maintain a positive attitude when people disappoint them and then need to be able to sustain their energy for the journey. This ability to bounce back and to persist is called resilience. Without this leaders too easily give up and without it they have not got the personal resources to motivate and energise their followers and teams.

**What this step means**

Leaders are inspired by the journey and are not derailed by adversity. They persist because they are able to keep the vision larger in their minds than the problems that they face. They focus on what they can do, not on what they can't. They are able to maintain their energy because when faced with hurdles they are still able to see the larger vision. It is their passion for the vision which keeps them energised. It is their ability to keep this sense of perspective that gives them the ability to bounce back and keep their focus on the journey. A large measure of their resilience comes from their sense of optimism. They are able to find the positives, as well as the negatives, in any situation and this helps them to keep things in perspective. They are not overwhelmed by the magnitude of the problems they encounter, as they see these as an inevitable consequence of progress and increased complexity.

**How this step has changed**

The pressures on leaders today means that they have to have good processes for personal renewal and for managing stress. They cannot afford stress to cloud their thinking and to create dysfunctional behaviour. A level of stress is a good thing as it energises and creates focus. It is when stress becomes over-whelming that it produces poor decisions and often impulsive responses. Leaders need to be able to take time out to reflect and step aside to see things in a broader perspective.

Leaders need to have healthy balance in life and be able to manage their priorities in both their personal and professional lives. Leaders today need to be conscious of their health and their social supports. They need a sensible diet and sufficient exercise to energise them through physically demanding days. Finally they need to be passionate about what they do and find what it is that brings fulfilment through their work.

**What this step means for you**

It means that you really need to understand what drives you and what you want to achieve in both your professional and personal life. You need to be clear about the difference you want to make and inspired by the challenge. It is the vision which has meaning for you personally, which will sustain you over time and nurture your resilience. It is clarity of vision that will energise you and help you to keep moving forward despite the obstacles and setbacks.

It means that you will need to make regular time to reflect and to review where you are going. It means that you will need, over time, to continually reinvigorate your vision by keeping it up to date with new ideas and by having a support network of mentors to discuss it with. Leaders are great networkers and the best are always making contacts and building relationships with key people in their extended environment. You will also need good feedback mechanisms to tell you when you are off track and making decisions which are not consistent with your values or your vision. You need to be aware of your stress levels and understand when your decisions are based on anxiety rather than your personal intent or long term agenda.

**What you can do:**

1.  Establish a positive routine

    Draw up a plan to have a regular routine which helps you to deal with stress. It should be something you enjoy doing that is relaxing and invigorating. It could be a neighbourhood walk, listening to music, finding a quiet place to think.

2.  Learn more about managing stress

    Read a book on stress management to better understand it, its impact and what can be done to deal with it. Look for ideas and practical strategies.

3. Adopt meditation

   Take a class in meditation or mindfulness to help you to learn how to calm and focus your mind. A class will provide a structured disciple for attendance but also provide the support required to adopt a new practice.

4. Take exercise

   Have a regular walk/run/cycle/swim to clear your head and to give you the energy to think clearly. If you are entering a stressful period you need to be fit and build reserves of energy to deal with increased demands.

5. Review your support network

   Think about the people in your support network and consider whether you are making sufficient time to build these relationships. Are you devoting sufficient time to sustaining and building your key relationships?

**A final reminder**

In a world of constant change, unexpected events and escalating challenges, leaders need to maintain their own personal resilience. You need to be able to sustain the journey and maintain the passion over time. You need to keep in shape for the long haul and not be hijacked by your own emotions or derailed by stress. Having a sense of perspective, a deep leadership purpose, keeping a healthy balance in life and maintaining a close personal network are all part of the process of keeping you fit to lead.

## Development plan for mastering this step: Building Resilience

### 1. What more do I need to know?

To take this step I need to know more about.....

### 2. What are the benefits of taking this step?

If I could master this step it would enable me to.....

### 3. What might make this hard to do?

The challenges I face in taking this step are.....

### 4. What would I have to change?

The behaviours I need to adopt to complete this step are.....

### 5. What might be some obstacles?

The things that might stop me from taking this step are.....

### 6. Where do I start?

The first thing I need to do to get started is to.....

### 7. What would help me to succeed?

The supports I would need to put in place to help me to take this step are.....

### 8. What would be the signs of success?

I would know I had been successful in taking this step when.....

# Part Two

# Team Leadership

If you decide that you want to lead others or are placed in a role where you are responsible for the development and performance of others then the steps of team leadership will be critical for you to master.

Wanting to step up to the leadership of a team doesn't mean that you necessarily want to be the centre of attention, but it does mean that you want to take charge, and accept ultimate responsibility for the performance of the team. It means that you are motivated to develop others and to help them to achieve their potential. It means that as a leader you are driven by team success and that you are prepared to challenge individuals and teams in order to achieve this. Team leaders today rely upon influence more than control, but are prepared to be directive when necessary to influence an outcome. The key point is not to take ownership away from the team. The focus is to make the team the star. The more the leader prescribes what is to be done and how it is to be done, the more ownership stays with the leader.

Team leadership is a style of leadership that is exercised through others. It is leadership that is directed through people, with a starting point that the leader is essentially in the service of the people being led. The leader is not satisfied with simply being part of a team, but is compelled to contribute to the performance and development of the team. The leader's role is to bring out the best in individuals and then help them to work together in ways that create their best possible team. This would be a team that is not only extremely successful, but is also personally satisfying to be in.

**There are seven steps to master:**

1. Leaders attract the right people – bring the people with the right skills and values into the team

2. Leaders get the best out of people – develop the potential of members of the team

3. Leaders build shared understanding – ensure understanding for all members of the team

4. Leaders give recognition to others – recognition and appreciation build engagement and performance

5. Leaders address performance issues – performance issues rarely improve on their own

6. Leaders inspire people – inspiration is a powerful way to awaken potential in people

7. Leaders help teams to succeed – build performance capabilities in the team

With a solid grounding in personal leadership, the next steps on the leadership journey are through team leadership and interpersonal influence. Once you have mastered your impact on others, you can then move to strategic leadership which is concerned with building a successful and sustainable organisation.

# Step eight:

# Leaders attract the right people

A leader's ability to attract talented people will be a key determinant of leadership success. Having a radar for quality people is a strength and will enable the leader to bring the right mix of people into a team. Once you attract people, then the challenge is to develop them and then retain them. Having an eye for talent is the start. One of the key secrets of exceptional leadership is seeing beyond what people are today, to what they might become tomorrow.

## What this step means

Leaders are careful about the people they recruit. They won't just allow anyone into the team. They would rather play one person short than have someone in the team who undermines the team. It is important to ensure that new recruits have not only the ability but also the passion to succeed. The simple proposition is that no one seeks to excel at something they are not passionate about. You have to ensure that new members are passionate about the things that matter most to the team so that there is strong alignment between what people want and what the team needs. Ensuring that there is alignment of values before you recruit is better than trying to change values once people are employed. Getting the right people is the key building block for team success.

## How this step has changed

In the past management was often just a numbers game. It was all too often simply getting people on the job and in the team. Little attention was given to getting the right people and there was scarcely any attention given to aligning the values of people with the values of the organisation. High performing organisations recognise that you are better off with no person than with the wrong person. They are aware of the negative impact of the wrong person on team morale and team performance. A simple test to determine if you have the wrong person is to judge whether the team functions better when that person is absent.

It means that leaders when they are recruiting need to ensure that people have not only the capabilities required to do the job, but more importantly have the values that align with the culture. Exceptional leaders seem to have an intuitive feel for this, but they also ask the right questions to validate that feel. They ask questions about past team experiences, about what the person is proud of and about what the person really wants to achieve. You can pick up a lot from how the questions are answered as well as what is said.

Terry Lee

## What this step means for you

It is important for leaders to understand their own values so they can better identify the values of others. It doesn't mean attracting people who have exactly the same values, but they must have enough shared values to build trust. In a strategic sense it also means that the leader must be aware of how his/her values align with the strategy or business principles and aware where there might be areas of tension or non-alignment. Leadership is not about having your friends in the team. Being friends with the people in your team is a good thing, but not always a necessary thing. Being friendly is more important than being friends. Being successful is the ultimate prize.

## What you can do:

1.  Review your recruitment

    Reflect on what you look for in the people you seek to recruit. Do you look for people who will challenge and who will complement the team skill set or simply people who will fit in with the team?

2.  Recall personal best teams

    Think about the best teams you have been in. How did they introduce people into the team and make them feel welcome? What did they do that made you feel included?

3.  Involve the team in recruiting

    Talk to your teams about what is important for them in a new team member. Consider attitude as well as ability as well as potential contribution. Involve the team in the recruitment process.

4.  Take care with induction

How you introduce new people to the team and how they begin sets in place an important pattern for subsequent team interactions. Take the time to prepare a well thought through and carefully structured induction process for new recruits, so that they get a fast start to your culture and expectations.

5. Align team values

Whilst you might look for complementarity in skills, it is important to look for people who have values alignment. Think about the values that are important for success at a personal and at a team level

## A final reminder

Getting the right people into the team is the foundation for success. As a leader your challenge is not filling seats it is ensuring that you are able to attract and recruit the right people. The goal is not recruiting people who think alike or people who will make your life easier. Don't forget that the most talented people are often the most difficult to manage because they have such high expectations. You have to accept that the better the people are, the better your leadership must be. The easiest people to manage are those with low expectations, because they don't expect much. In return however they don't give much.

### Development plan for mastering this step: Attracting the Right People

**1.  What more do I need to know?**

To take this step I need to know more about.....

**2. What are the benefits of taking this step?**

If I could master this step it would enable me to.....

**3. What might make this hard to do?**

The challenges I face in taking this step are.....

**4. What would I have to change?**

The behaviours I need to adopt to complete this step are.....

### 5. What might be some obstacles?

The things that might stop me from taking this step are.....

### 6. Where do I start?

The first thing I need to do to get started is to.....

### 7. What would help me to succeed?

The supports I would need to put in place to help me to take this step are.....

### 8. What would be the signs of success?

I would know I had been successful in taking this step when.....

# Step nine:

# Leaders get the best out of people

The key battleground in a competitive business environment is the one fought with the skills and capabilities of the people deployed. In a rapidly changing environment, where innovation is the key, sustainable success is derived by unlocking the potential of the workforce. The future for our organisations, and for our communities, is not the ordinary, it is the potential that comes from people working together to do the extra-ordinary. It is what we might achieve, but have yet to achieve, that holds the future for human progress. Great leaders inspire people to go beyond what they think is possible.

## What this step means

Effective leaders build relationships which generate greater discretionary effort. Discretionary effort is the effort that people put into their work over and above what they are required to do. The best organisations have leaders who are able to get more from their people, more often and more consistently. It is the relationships with the leader that is critical. The way that people are treated is a key driver of the satisfaction that they feel at work, and it is the degree of satisfaction that sustains the effort they put in day in and day out.

## How this step has changed

Organisations in the past had enough trouble just getting people to do what they were required to do. Today doing your job is expected and it is the organisations that are able to find ways to get more from their people that have the edge. It's not about working longer hours, but giving people a reason to do more while they are at work. It's going the extra mile, contributing to discussions, supporting colleagues, bringing positive energy and listening carefully to what customers say. We now know that this has a lot to do with the culture that it is created, but we also now that it is specifically related to how they are led.

As competitive pressures increase and strategic challenges constantly emerge, it will be the organisations that can continually develop their people that will survive. Those that are agile, adaptable and grow talent will thrive. Every team today whether in sport or in business has a salary cap. You cannot just get improved performance by putting more people on the team. It is getting more from the people on the team that is the answer. Finding the key to unlock this potential is the challenge.

## What this step means for you

It means that as a leader you have to be a student of human motivation and performance. A good place to start is with reflection upon what it is that motivates you to do your best and what is it in the environment that brings this out. Equally, it is useful to think about people, places and situations that have the opposite affect and cause you to lose interest and motivation. Creating a climate for success and the right conditions to get the best out of people is a major focus for leaders and because we are so different it often doing means different things for different people. Like the coach of a football team the leader has to find the trigger for each person which will stimulate his/her growth and development and will enable him/her to make their greatest contribution to the overall team's success.

## What you can do:

1. Build a climate for development

Reflect on the climate that is present in the team. Is it a climate that stimulates learning and development? Are team members inspired to be the best they can be?

2. Build a high performance team

Think about the great teams that you have known, where people worked together to produce results far beyond what individuals working alone could have produced. What was it that made those teams so good?

3. Understand team motivation

Think about the people in your team. What drives them at work and what is it that they are really looking for? What is it that motivates their drive for personal best and energises them to do their best work?

4.   Development plans for team members

Draw up a specific development plan for each team member. Consider how to make it personal, relevant and challenging. Ensure that it not only helps the individual to grow in personal capability, but also in the capability to make a greater contribution to team success.

5.   Model the way

What you do will always be a more powerful message than what you say, and how you show you learn will have a greater impact then what you teach. Demonstrate your own commitment to personal best through the goals you set and the way you deliver.


**A final reminder**

Many organisations have difficulty just getting people to do the job they are paid to do.  Think about the environment that gets the best out of you and think about the way you need to treat people to get the best out of them.  The best teams are those that are satisfying to be in and produce the best results.  Be a student of human motivation and performance and think about what it takes to get the best out of people.  Think about the difference between the average groups you have been in and the high performing teams you have experienced. Leaders have a significant impact on the development and performance of the people and teams that they lead.

## Development plan for mastering this step: Getting the Best out of People

### 1. What more do I need to know?

To take this step I need to know more about......

### 2. What are the benefits of taking this step?

If I could master this step it would enable me to......

### 3. What might make this hard to do?

The challenges I face in taking this step are......

### 4. What would I have to change?

The behaviours I need to adopt to complete this step are......

### 5. What might be some obstacles?

The things that might stop me from taking this step are.....

### 6. Where do I start?

The first thing I need to do to get started is to.....

### 7. What would help me to succeed?

The supports I would need to put in place to help me to take this step are.....

### 8. What would be the signs of success?

I would know I had been successful in taking this step when.....

# Step ten:

# Leaders build shared understanding

Communication is complex and influence is always a challenge. Teams today can no longer be dependent and totally reliant on the boss for direction or decisions. Leaders must ensure that people and teams understand what is expected of them, understand how to make effective decisions and understand the impact of their actions and decisions. Just telling people does not ensure that they understand. Sometimes what you thought you said is not what people heard and understood. Never assume that people "just get it". Always check to make sure.

## What this step means

Leaders have to find ways to explain to people what is happening, why it is happening and what they are going to do about it. It is not helpful to provide complex or obscure diagrams, frameworks or messages. Leaders have to strip away the complexity to find the essence. Simple, not simplistic, messages are the key to focus. When things get complex, people can get confused and this then leads to anxiety and this in the long run causes a drop in performance. Creating understanding is a key leadership task and leaders do this by telling stories and by building explanatory frameworks and models which help people to understand how the world has changed, appreciate how decisions are made and results are achieved.

## How this step has changed

In the past it was common practice for leaders to keep their people uninformed. Organisations expected compliance and simply following rules required very little understanding. The problem is that this approach led to a very passive workforce with a high level of dependency on the boss. The result was that people were, in essence, encouraged to do just what they were required to do and no more. It didn't produce discretionary effort and it didn't encourage initiative, and it virtually ruled out innovation and learning.

The focus on building performance cultures meant that this simple minded approach was no longer appropriate. Performance is built upon discretionary effort, initiative and execution. Empowerment which is a core practice of this approach means that if you are to hold people accountable then they need to understand what they are accountable for and understand the impact of what they do. If they are to have the autonomy to make decisions, then they need to understand the basis upon which decisions are made, and appreciate the consequences of decisions taken. The new empowered, agile and responsive organisations of today demand leaders who can build understanding, especially at the frontline and especially in interactions with the customers.

## What this step means for you

A major task of leaders is to explain, to teach and to create understanding. It means that you cannot just assume that "people get it". You have to find ways to make things that are complex as simple as possible. It means that you will have to think about the ways that you can simplify things as far as possible without being simplistic and losing the essential meaning. Making things simplistic is to talk down to people, whereas taking the time to explain is to treat them with respect. Your ability to articulate and to explain complex subjects, and the ability to be able to see things from another's perspective, will be fundamental to your capacity to influence others and to create understanding.

## What you can do:

1. Make the complex simple

   Reflect on the complex issues and business models your team needs to understand. Find explanatory frameworks to make things as simple as possible. The key is to make them simple, without making them simplistic.

2. Gain insight into team thinking

   Ask your team challenging questions and listen to how people interpret and explain. This will give insight into their thinking and level of understanding. Listening before telling, asking before directing, is the key to this step.

3. Have better, deeper conversations

   Have regular conversations with people you respect about some of the complex issues facing leaders today. Learn from what we have done before, and clarify what we might do in the future. Be curious about the world and read widely to gain different perspectives.

4. Learn from others

   Pay attention when others speak to observe how they explain issues and to identify opportunities for your own development. Seek people you respect and wish to learn from.

5. Be an active learner in your own development

   After a discussion ask for feedback about how well you explained an issue or concept and what you might do next time to be more effective. Always look for ways to explain complex matters more simply and more effectively.

**A final reminder**

As the world gets more complex and uncertain leaders need to bring clarity and meaning. Explaining what is happening, and why it is happening, and what we intend to do about it is a key leadership challenge. If you want to empower people or want them to use their initiative or if you want to rely upon their judgement then you need to understand how they think. You also have to involve them in the explanation so that you get thoughtful understanding not superficial acceptance. You want informed consent, not blind compliance. So leaders need to be informed, know how to facilitate discussion, and then have a process for getting shared understanding and agreement.

## Development plan for mastering this step: Building Shared Understanding

### 1. What more do I need to know?

To take this step I need to know more about.....

### 2. What are the benefits of taking this step?

If I could master this step it would enable me to.....

### 3. What might make this hard to do?

The challenges I face in taking this step are.....

### 4. What would I have to change?

The behaviours I need to adopt to complete this step are.....

## 5. What might be some obstacles?

The things that might stop me from taking this step are.....

## 6. Where do I start?

The first thing I need to do to get started is to.....

## 7. What would help me to succeed?

The supports I would need to put in place to help me to take this step are.....

## 8. What would be the signs of success?

I would know I had been successful in taking this step when.....

# Step eleven:

# Leaders give recognition to others

Everyone wants to feel that his/her efforts are appreciated. At a basic level people want to be noticed and to feel valued. At a higher level they want to have impact and to feel that they can make a difference. When people are ignored they are effectively shut out of a relationship and their sense of worth can suffer. Leaders need to build the confidence of the people they lead. They do this by paying attention to people's needs, supporting them in their development and showing appreciation for what they do. Leaders give recognition to build confidence and trust.

## What this step means

Leaders give recognition to the people they lead. It is the leader's job to put the spotlight on others and to draw them forward and to build their confidence. It is not the leader's role to dominate the spotlight, except when there is a specific requirement to do so. The leader's job is to build the team and to develop the individuals in the team. Leaders do this by giving recognition, providing feedback and expressing appreciation for the contribution of others. In this way they build the self esteem and sense of worth in others and this helps them to develop the resilience required to sustain change in tough and uncertain times.

## How this step has changed

Recognition is a primary mechanism that we use to build the self esteem of others and to show them that they are important. It is a way that we signify their worth and it is a way that we show that we value the contribution that they make. Recognition is a very personal thing and the way that we give recognition is also influenced by cultural considerations. For example the way you give recognition in China will be different to what you might do in Australia and what works well in the U.S. may not work elsewhere.

Recognition is the way we show our appreciation and respect for others. It can be a personal expression of gratitude for what someone has done. It might also be paying tribute to someone publicly in a speech. It might be a hand shake or a hug, and it could be a letter or a gift. Whatever it is must be relevant to the person and appropriate to the situation. When it is unexpected it is more powerful and leaders should be looking for opportunities to provide spontaneous recognition. When it becomes an expectation it loses its surprise and its impact.

Whatever way it is given recognition is a prime mechanism that leaders use for building trust, for motivating behaviour and for building self esteem and confidence. Finding ways to do this with a diverse workforce and with globally dispersed teams is an on-going challenge for leaders today.

## What this step means for you

It means that leaders have to be genuinely interested in people and especially in the people that they lead. It means that they cannot be simply interested in their own goals and objectives but must be prepared to pay attention to the development needs of others. Good leaders seek to "put the spotlight" on others and their achievements and do not seek to attract the attention and praise for themselves. It means that as a leader you have to be prepared to say "we" rather than "I" and say "us" rather than "me". It does not mean that you have to be an extravert, but it does mean that you have to make it a priority to pay attention and give recognition to the contribution and achievements of others. Those who are introverts can provide sincere recognition but they often have to structure themselves in order to do it consistently.

## What you can do:

1. Use the power of authentic recognition

   Reflect on how often you give recognition or show appreciation for the support of another person. You may not need a lot of recognition yourself but this does not mean that others don't. Recognition that is personal and authentic is powerful in building trust and self-esteem.

2. Be grateful for support

   Remember that a lot of people have helped you on your journey and supported you to get to where you are today. Make a list of the people who have helped you and still help you to deal with challenges and contribute to your success. Note down what it is that you are thankful for or appreciate most about them.

3. Give credit where it is due

   Make a call or write a note to thank people for their support. You don't need a particular reason to say thanks, just the ability to reach out and communicate your appreciation in a personal, respectful way.

4. Actively maintain your network

   Make contact with people who are important to you that you have not spoken to for some time. Find out what is happening in their lives and potentially find out what support they might need from you.

5. Look for positive examples

   Look for examples of recognition given to people in the organisations you visit. Look at the impact of formal and informal ways, and the impact of individual and group recognition.

## A final reminder

Everyone wants to feel appreciated and to feel that their efforts are noticed. It is a basic human need to feel valued. People are different in the way they want to receive recognition and leaders need to do it in a way that is sincere yet productive. You need to use your judgement. Giving recognition too freely or where it is unwarranted devalues it. It needs to be given regularly but selectively. Think about how you like to receive recognition yourself, but appreciate that not everyone is like you. Many leaders are very self confident and don't seek much feedback themselves. Be aware that just because you don't need much recognition, doesn't mean that other people don't. On the other hand, too much recognition can be perceived as insincere. As a leader it is good to be generous of spirit and to make it a habit to regularly seek opportunities to express appreciation to others.

## Development plan for mastering this step: Giving Recognition to Others

### 1. What more do I need to know?

To take this step I need to know more about.....

### 2. What are the benefits of taking this step?

If I could master this step it would enable me to.....

### 3. What might make this hard to do?

The challenges I face in taking this step are.....

### 4. What would I have to change?

The behaviours I need to adopt to complete this step are.....

### 5. What might be some obstacles?

The things that might stop me from taking this step are.....

### 6. Where do I start?

The first thing I need to do to get started is to.....

### 7. What would help me to succeed?

The supports I would need to put in place to help me to take this step are.....

### 8. What would be the signs of success?

I would know I had been successful in taking this step when.....

# Step twelve

# Leaders address performance issues

The ability to perform and to get results consistently over time is the mark of an exceptional team. Leaders need to appreciate that whilst building self esteem and confidence in others is crucial, it is often team success which has the greatest impact on these two. Leaders must be pro-active in setting performance standards and in building high performing teams. A large part of this is ensuring that performance expectations are clear and that non-performance is addressed. There may be situational or strategic reasons for it but underlying performance issues rarely spontaneously improve. Allowing people to fail is not good leadership.

## What this step means

Leaders do not leave problems unattended and they do not take the easy option of passing the problem to someone else. They know that to nip a problem in the bud is the best option and that whilst it might cause some angst initially is a lot easier to resolve than allowing a problem to become part of a person's habitual behaviour. Problems in performance and problems in interpersonal relationships rarely correct themselves and if they are left unattended they inevitably produce deep seated resentments and friction. Leaders see it as part of their professional responsibility to drive performance. They do this by setting expectations, giving feedback and by coaching people to improve what they do.

## How this step has changed

There was a time when managers were more concerned with compliance than performance. This was time when doing what you were told, as you were told, and when you were told was the fundamental expectation of workers. Doing it well was a bonus and doing it right was a requirement. This approach worked well at a time when business strategies were "more of the same" and "business as usual" was the norm. But it didn't work well in a more competitive global business environment when the ability to perform was paramount.

Performance pressures were placed on organisations as expectations began to rise. Investors began to look for better than average returns, customers were looking for greater value and service, and the new employees in the age of the "war for talent" were looking for employers who would challenge them, develop them, respect them and then reward them well. What this has meant is that there is a demand for leaders who will invest time and energy in building the performance capabilities of the people they lead. This calls for leaders who set performance expectations, and build the capabilities required to succeed.

In a world of rapid change organisations need a great deal of strategic agility if they are to adapt and survive. Whilst strategic agility is crucial, it must be built upon some core capabilities. Strategy without capability is a dream. It is the capabilities that turn an idea into a plan for action, and it is leaders at all levels in organisations who build the capabilities that enable well thought through strategies to succeed.

In fact it is the strength and breadth of capabilities that provide the flexibility for serious strategic thinking. If capabilities are thin then so too will strategic options be limited.

**What this step means for you**

It means that as a leader you have to be firm but fair, demanding yet supportive. As a leader you have to be tough on non performance and not accept second best. Leaders are driven to excel and they expect the best from the people they lead. It means that some leaders who have great empathy for people need to toughen up, and at the same time it means that leaders who are uncompromising on performance need to do so in a way which is sensitive and supportive.

It means that leaders need to apply the same standards firstly to themselves. They need to be demanding of their own performance so that they can model their passion to succeed to others. Holding yourself accountable for what you do and delivering on what you promise are base line attributes of leadership. Walking the talk is the best way to set the right example.

**What you can do:**

1. Be a role model for performance

   Reflect on the extent to which you demonstrate a commitment to high performance and the extent to which people would see that you have a passion for your own personal development. Do you also challenge people about increasing the contribution they make to the team?

2.  Take pride in your performance

    Lists your own achievements of which you are especially proud. What made these so special? Outline what it took from you to achieve these things and what were the capabilities required. Describe what these examples have taught you about achievement and your own personal values.

3.  Challenge people to perform

    Don't walk away from performance issues. What do you need to do, or stop doing, to help people in your team to be more successful? Leaders challenge people to be excellent.

4.  Prepare specific performance development plans

    Have a discussion with the people in your team about the challenges they face and their needs for development. Performance needs both attitude and ability and leaders need to work on both at all times.

5.  Build your skill base

    Take a course in performance development or an applied coaching workshop. Make a commitment to being excellent at developing talent and unlocking potential.

## A final reminder

Leadership is not about enshrining the status quo and it is certainly not about keeping people where they are. Leaders are catalysts for change. Leadership is all about change and development and taking people to the future. This means that leaders have to be change agents and people developers and have to invest time and energy in building capabilities and in improving performance. It means that as a leader it is necessary to have a strong commitment to your own personal development and you need to apply daily discipline to continually seeking ways to improve your own performance and practice.

## Development plan for mastering this step: Addressing Performance Issues

### 1. What more do I need to know?

To take this step I need to know more about.....

### 2. What are the benefits of taking this step?

If I could master this step it would enable me to.....

### 3. What might make this hard to do?

The challenges I face in taking this step are.....

### 4. What would I have to change?

The behaviours I need to adopt to complete this step are.....

### 5. What might be some obstacles?

The things that might stop me from taking this step are.....

### 6. Where do I start?

The first thing I need to do to get started is to.....

### 7. What would help me to succeed?

The supports I would need to put in place to help me to take this step are.....

### 8. What would be the signs of success?

I would know I had been successful in taking this step when.....

# Step thirteen:

# Leaders inspire people

To inspire others is to awaken in them the possibility of a better future. It is to give them belief in their greater potential and give them the energy to break through the barriers to achieving that potential. Leaders can motivate people to act in a certain way and to focus on certain priorities. This is called extrinsic motivation and is motivation that comes from outside of the person through rewards or incentives. The greatest gift that leaders give to the people they lead is through stimulating intrinsic motivation which is the motivation that comes from within and is directed towards fulfilling one's own dreams and potential. Inspiration is a powerful force for change and for growth and development.

## What this step means

The greatest expectation of leaders is that they inspire the people they lead. Leaders inspire people with the vision and what is possible. They bring hope and a greater confidence in the future. They give people the belief that they can do great things and they breathe life into the aspirations that they have. It is inspiration that people most want to see in their leaders and it is unfortunately too often the quality that is least found. In order to inspire others, leaders need to be inspired themselves, and it is this passion expressed which has such a contagious impact on the people they lead.

## How this step has changed

Inspiration is in demand today especially in developed economies because people are looking for more than simply a job. People now want to make a difference through their work. They want to feel that they have contributed to something greater and what inspirational leaders do is to bring significance to the work of the individual. That is, the leader shows the individual the significance of what he or she does in contributing to the overall result or to the vision. The inspiration comes from the belief in self and the passion in purpose that is stimulated, nurtured and realised. Leaders increasingly need to connect people and their dreams to the visions and goals of the organisations in which they work. In this work they need to be astute at understanding people but also adept at bringing the vision to life in a very practical way.

## What this step means for you

It means that as a leader you have to know what drives you and at a deeper level understand the dreams and aspirations you harbour. It is being in touch with the things that inspire you that will produce the passion and purpose that is so evident in inspirational leaders. It is not salesmanship, although it is important to be a good communicator. Neither is it charisma. What inspires people is a leader who has a genuine belief in their development and in their potential to do great things. Leaders are people who passionately believe in what they do and have the determination to see it through. Understanding what you have come to do as a leader is an important pre-requisite for exceptional leadership.

**What you can do:**

1. Review your personal inspiration

   Reflect on what it is that you are inspired to do. Think about what brings energy and personal satisfaction to your work and to your life. Consider what you can do to sustain your inspiration and to re-energise yourself when times are tough.

2. Identify inspiring leaders

   Think about leaders you have met who have inspired you. What was it they did? How did they influence what you thought and what you felt?

3. Align your personal and organisational goals

   Consider how much time you give to ensure that your personal goals and the organisation's goals are really aligned? Make a list of the key drivers of satisfaction in your work?

4. Bring passion and energy

   Reflect upon the things that you are really passionate about achieving. How much do these passions energise you and influence your mood and how you interact at work?

5. Mix with people who inspire you

   Find a mentor or colleagues who share your passion. Make a regular time to catch up and talk about how you can bring a greater sense of purpose and passion to your work.

## A final reminder

Inspiration is a powerful force in human motivation and is a powerful driver of human achievement. It is also something that brings passion to leadership and creates a strong emotional connection between leader, follower and vision. Inspiration is concerned with making a difference and contributing to something worthwhile. It brings energy to human endeavour and sustains people even on the darkest days.

Inspiration is more enduring that extrinsic motivation and is a great source for the resilience required to lead in a challenging world. Knowing what inspires you as a leader brings a great strength to your leadership and knowing what you are inspired to do makes it easy to set daily priorities. When leaders lose their inspiration they lose the passion to lead and they either need to find it or move on.

# Development plan for mastering this step: Inspiring People

**1. What more do I need to know?**

To take this step I need to know more about......

**2. What are the benefits of taking this step?**

If I could master this step it would enable me to......

**3. What might make this hard to do?**

The challenges I face in taking this step are......

**4. What would I have to change?**

The behaviours I need to adopt to complete this step are......

### 5. What might be some obstacles?

The things that might stop me from taking this step are.....

### 6. Where do I start?

The first thing I need to do to get started is to.....

### 7. What would help me to succeed?

The supports I would need to put in place to help me to take this step are.....

### 8. What would be the signs of success?

I would know I had been successful in taking this step when.....

# Step fourteen:

# Leaders help teams to succeed

Leaders are given to the team for the team's sake. Teams are not given to the leader for the leader's sake. The challenge for team leaders is to put leadership into the team, not to take it out. It is to add value to the team, by stimulating its development and challenging it to achieve excellence. Leaders need to understand the external context within which the team operates and to identify the stakeholders and what they expect. Leaders need to challenge and develop the individuals within the team and to help them to be active constructive contributors to team success.

## What this step means

Leaders make the team the star and they understand that the ultimate test of their leadership, and of the value they bring is the contribution they make to team satisfaction and success. Leaders think about what is required from them to take the team to the next stage of development and up to the next level of performance. Leaders are continually taking the team on a journey from where they are today, to where they need to be tomorrow. When leaders have a wide repertoire of behaviours and practices they can be more selective in choosing the one that is most appropriate for the situation and the person.

## How this step has changed

It is the value that the leader brings to others and to the team which is a true indicator of their effectiveness. The team does not exist for the benefit of the leader. Rather the leader is in the service of the team. Certainly teams exist to deliver the organisational goals and thus the leader's objectives, but they can only do this to the extent that the leader builds their performance.

The biggest shift in team development today is for leaders to move beyond just participation in teams to contribution in teams. It is no longer sufficient that people are in teams and that they actively participate in the team. The crucial difference in successful teams is the contribution individuals make to the effectiveness of the team. It is what they do, that makes the difference, and what they don't do which is sometimes more important.

An effective leader is concerned to increase the capacity of each team member to contribute to team outcomes. The leader does this by making team members aware of what they do that helps the team and what they do that inhibits. They coach and give feedback and seek the triggers that release the potential that enables a group of people to become a real team.

## What this means step for you

It means that as a leader you must be certain about what you do that adds value to the team. This means that team building skills are important, but that team contribution skills are more important. It means being prepared to receive feedback yourself and to modify your behaviour in response. It means deliberately building team influencing skills and having the discipline to invest in the elimination of any team disrupting behaviours. It means investing in conflict management skills, in skills for collaboration and in effective listening and communication skills.

As a leader you need to appreciate the context within which the team operates and this means understanding competing external demands and expectations as well as being able to identify and work with a diverse range of stakeholders. Concern for building the team follows from a careful understanding of the strategic challenges faced by the team.

## What you can do:

1. Reflect on the makings of a great team

   Reflect on the great teams that you have been in. Great teams are ones that not only achieve great results, but are also personally satisfying to be in. What made these teams work so well and how did members feel about being in the team?

2. Build your own team leadership

   You can only help the team if you are an effective leader of the team. The best team leaders build leadership capability in the team, they don't make the team reliant on them. Review your own style in leading the team. What do you need to do to step up to a higher level of team leadership? What do you need to stop doing that is inhibiting the team from taking greater responsibility for leadership?

3. Develop a stakeholder map

   The success of a team occurs outside of the team, not within the team. Managing stakeholders and delivering on expectations are critical. Complete a strategic map of key stakeholders for the team. What do they expect and how strong are the team's relationships with them? What can the team do to build greater levels of trust?

4. Assess your personal team contribution

   Consider a great team that you were in – one that was highly satisfying and successful. Think about a time when you were most effective at contributing to this team's performance. What was happening and what was it you did?

5. Look to great role models

   Who do you know who are great role models and leaders you can learn from? Talk to leaders you admire as team builders and ask them for their secrets of success. Ask for advice on the challenges you face.

**A final reminder**

Leading a team is really taking that team to the future. It is building the skills and capabilities and confidence of individuals and showing them how to exercise these in the best interests of the team. Leaders must be able to manage their ego and understand that the real focus is not on them but on the team. They must make what is their own self-interest subservient to the interests of the team.

To do this, leaders need to appreciate the strategic context within which the team operates as well as have insight into the personal and interpersonal dynamics within the team. All teams exist within a context with their own specific strategic challenges. To really contribute to team performance you need to understand both the internal and external challenges and dynamics for the team.

## Development plan for mastering this step: Helping Teams to Succeed

### 1.  What more do I need to know?

To take this step I need to know more about.....

### 2. What are the benefits of taking this step?

If I could master this step it would enable me to.....

### 3. What might make this hard to do?

The challenges I face in taking this step are.....

### 4. What would I have to change?

The behaviours I need to adopt to complete this step are.....

## 5. What might be some obstacles?

The things that might stop me from taking this step are.....

## 6. Where do I start?

The first thing I need to do to get started is to.....

## 7. What would help me to succeed?

The supports I would need to put in place to help me to take this step are.....

## 8. What would be the signs of success?

I would know I had been successful in taking this step when.....

Terry Lee

# Part Three

# Strategic Leadership

If you decide that you want to move into a more strategic role, and have a long term impact on an organisation, then you must master the steps to strategic leadership.

Strategic leadership is the ability to contribute to the development and growth of an organisation, and at the same time position it for future success. It involves understanding the dynamics of organisational life and the factors that drive organisational success. It means appreciating the unique psychology of the organisation concerned and how issues are considered and decisions are made. Every organisation has its own particular culture which determines the way things are done. This culture is manifested in the behaviours of people and teams and these in turn are an expression of the underlying values at work. Strategic leaders understand this and appreciate that culture and strategy must be tightly aligned to achieve superior performance.

Strategic leaders are inspired by vision and are able to discern strategies which will create pathways for success. They can then build cultures which support this process. They are able to put in place structures which build cross functional collaboration and which drive consistent execution at all levels. Their understanding of organisational dynamics enables them to find ways to utilise the full resources available to them. It is their passion for change and their relentless quest to find ways to be more efficient and more effective that makes them especially valuable to their organisations.

**There are seven steps to master:**

1. Leaders develop shared vision – shared vision creates strong emotional connection and engagement

2. Leaders build performance cultures – performance cultures breed excellence

3. Leaders change mindsets – the major challenge is changing how people think

4. Leaders unlock the hidden value in people and teams – the greatest opportunity is the as yet unrealised potential

5. Leaders embrace learning and drive change – leaders must challenge the status quo

6. Leaders set a positive example – leaders are powerful role models

7. Leaders have a clear strategic agenda – leaders bring clarity and focus

Mastering strategic leadership gives you the ability to not only build organisations that are good for the people who work within them, but also good for the customers and communities that they serve and for the investors who look for a return on their funds.. By mastering personal, team and strategic leadership you can make the greatest contribution to others and make the greatest difference through your life and through your work.

# Step fifteen:

# Leaders develop shared vision

Developing a clear, worthwhile vision with the team is a powerful way to engage and align the individuals within and an effective way to ensure that all teams in the organisation are moving in the same direction. When leaders try to sell their vision to the team they are the one providing all of the energy and they are the one ultimately who retains the ownership. When the vision comes from the team, ownership is assumed by the team, and the energy that is required for performance or change is likely to be distributed across the individuals within the team. The team members will always work harder for their own idea than an idea that is imposed upon them. The leader can set the challenge and create the context for the vision, but must facilitate a process that enables the team to craft a shared vision.

## What this step means

Sharing the vision is the way to get people aligned and to create ownership. No one will work as hard for your vision as they will for their vision. Connecting the work that people do to the vision is a good way to build ownership. When people feel that what they do makes a difference, it brings a great deal of significance to the work that they do. It makes them feel that they have a personal role to play in achieving success and creating the future.

Having defined goals can certainly motivate and influence the choices that people make, but it is having a compelling vision that can truly inspire. Sharing a vision involves communicating both the conceptual content of the vision as well as the emotional appeal. The connection that people have to the vision is cognitive and emotional and ultimately behavioural.

## How this step has changed

There was a time when the leader was the boss and people were expected to do what they were told. Today we understand that enrolling people in a vision is the best way to create ownership. Having a shared vision becomes a crucial foundation for getting traction with strategic priorities at the frontline. If people are not guided by a sense of vision then they will just be doing what they are directed to do and there is no discretionary effort in that.

It is also crucial today to ensure that the senior leadership team shares a common vision; not only of what they expect from the organisation but also what the organisation can expect of them. How the leadership team behaves sends a powerful message down into the organisation about the culture and what behaviours are appropriate and what behaviours are not. A shared vision is also the basis for collaboration across an organisation and for eliminating the "silo mentality" and the "not my problem" attitude that often impedes organisational performance.

## What this step means for you

Whilst having a vision is the first step, being able to share that with others comes next. This means that you need to be comfortable talking about what inspires you and finding different ways to express it, whether through stories or examples or pictures. It helps people to understand you and what motivates you and makes your communications with them much more personal. It doesn't mean bragging about your vision or what you want to achieve. It just means sincerely and genuinely telling people a little more about yourself and what you hope for. Sharing vision is an important skill to develop and it will be a key leadership strength as you continue your leadership journey.

## What you can do:

1. Assess how well do you listen

   Reflect upon how well you listen, how well you challenge and how often you show a genuine interest in the thoughts and ideas of others.

2. Share your dreams

   Begin telling people about what you are trying to achieve through your work. It doesn't have to be a speech. In fact it is better if it is informal and expressed in your own words. Something that comes from the heart is more memorable than delivering someone else's speech.

3. Show a genuine interest other people's ideas

   Start asking people what they are motivated to do. Show a genuine interest in their goals and dreams. Ask them what they enjoy about their work and the people they work with.

4. Get people involved in vision creation

Have a process to include people in the development of shared vision. Make sure they can see through the process and in the final product that their thoughts and ideas and even words are included.

5. Generate interest in the future

Keep people informed about the future and stimulate their thinking about the trends that are shaping your industry. Get people excited about what is possible.

## A final reminder

Sharing a vision with someone else is a way to build a strong relationship and a mutual connection with something important. A vision is more than an objective or a goal. These can be important in setting a direction, and in establishing priorities for action, but alone they will never have the degree of inspiration and produce the amount of energy that a compelling vision can. A vision is something worthwhile that creates possibility, and stimulates a sense of purpose related to a dream outcome. All great things are achieved by people with a strong belief. Having a belief that is worthwhile stimulates human progress. Learning how to build shared vision is the way to harness human energy, passion and imagination and is fundamental to performance and growth in teams and organisations.

## Development plan for mastering this step: Developing Shared Vision

**1. What more do I need to know?**
To take this step I need to know more about.....

**2. What are the benefits of taking this step?**
If I could master this step it would enable me to.....

**3. What might make this hard to do?**
The challenges I face in taking this step are.....

**4. What would I have to change?**
The behaviours I need to adopt to complete this step are.....

## 5. What might be some obstacles?

The things that might stop me from taking this step are.....

## 6. Where do I start?

The first thing I need to do to get started is to.....

## 7. What would help me to succeed?

The supports I would need to put in place to help me to take this step are.....

## 8. What would be the signs of success?

I would know I had been successful in taking this step when.....

# Step sixteen:

# Leaders build performance cultures

Culture is the energy that powers the strategy. There is no point in having a five star strategy if it is being powered by a one star culture, because the strategy will only be executed to the extent that the people through the culture deliver it. Strategy is important because it brings clarity and focus and helps organisations to align key initiatives. The culture brings people together, helps them to perform at their best and provides them with the ownership to be accountable for results. Culture is the X factor which breeds success, and it is the role of the leader to build a performance culture that drives better outcomes.

## What this step means

Leaders must build a culture which will support the strategy of the team. In fact the strategy will only be effective to the extent that the culture supports and drives it. Strategic thinking is nothing more than wishful thinking if the culture does not support it. The culture needs to ensure high levels of engagement and ownership, because this is what ensures that people perform at their best. It is the example that the leaders set, the behaviour that they model, that has the single greatest impact on culture. The culture in any organisation is a consequence of years of behaviour by leaders at all levels who on a daily basis reinforce "the way things are done around here".

Leaders must be clear about the culture they are trying to build and then behave accordingly. Leaders can no longer come to the office and do what ever they want to do, display whatever behaviour they like. A leader today has a professional responsibility to be the leader the organisation needs and that the people require.

## How this step has changed

Very little attention was given to corporate culture in the past and it is only since the 1990's that we have appreciated its impact on performance. Now the evidence is clear that culture has a significant impact on performance. All organisations globally devote considerable time, resources and energy to the challenge of building culture and changing culture. Whilst the strategy is crucial in setting direction, the culture will determine the extent to which it is executed. For example, a strategy of excellence will never be delivered in a culture that doesn't value personal best and a strategy that relies on innovation will not succeed without a strong culture of learning. The culture underpins the strategy and is at the heart of each team interaction and every customer experience.

## What this step means for you

It means that leaders need to understand the power of culture and appreciate how cultures form and how they change. A great many organisations have ended up with cultures by default. That is, cultures they neither intended nor designed. Organisations that run into trouble usually find that their cultures are no longer relevant and in many cases are dysfunctional. This is usually due to long years of neglect and insufficient understanding of past leaders about the nature of culture and the impact it has. As a leader focus on the influence of culture in your family or in your club or association and become sensitive to the sometimes subtle, sometimes not so subtle, ways it influences behaviour and decision-making. Pay attention to culture and develop insight into the way different cultures have different processes and outcomes. Take care to design the culture that is right for you.

**What you can do:**

1.  Design a high performance culture

    What type of culture do you need to support your team's vision and strategy? How can you bring the values to life in a way that influences behaviour?

2.  Assess current reality

    Assess the culture as it is and the culture that would be necessary for superior performance. Consider the gap and think about what would need to change to narrow the gap.

3.  Build high levels of trust

    High performance cultures need high levels of trust. Team members need trust not only in other people but also in the systems, processes and strategies of the team. Make a list of the factors and behaviours that build trust in an organisation or team. Is it the same factors and behaviours that build trust in personal relationships?

Have a discussion with your peers or colleagues about this.

4.  Be open and transparent

    Coach team members in giving and receiving feedback as this is crucial in building high performance. Encourage teams to have open communication and to adopt transparent processes so that everyone can see how decisions are made. Look at members of the team and see if their behaviours reflects these values.

5.  Assess how people enter the team

    Review the processes and systems we use to bring people into the team. From the start, do we take the time to set people up for success in achieving results and embracing the culture of the team?

## A final reminder

Put a group of people together working on some task and in a short while they will have created a culture. Put them together for a longer time and they will have embedded this culture into the cultural fabric of the organisation. If they have some early success the culture they create will become resistant to change and they will believe that it contains the seeds of their current and future success. In the past we didn't pay much attention to getting the culture right, most attention was focussed on getting the strategy right. As a consequence many organisations ended up with cultures that were unproductive and that proved difficult to change. The irony was that many of these cultures didn't support the strategies that were adopted. We understand today that you cannot have high performance outcomes without a high performance culture, irrespective of your strategy. Having the skills to build these cultures is a basic expectation of effective leadership.

## Development plan for mastering this step: Building Performance Cultures

### 1. What more do I need to know?
To take this step I need to know more about.....

### 2. What are the benefits of taking this step?
If I could master this step it would enable me to.....

### 3. What might make this hard to do?
The challenges I face in taking this step are.....

### 4. What would I have to change?
The behaviours I need to adopt to complete this step are.....

### 5. What might be some obstacles?

The things that might stop me from taking this step are.....

### 6. Where do I start?

The first thing I need to do to get started is to.....

### 7. What would help me to succeed?

The supports I would need to put in place to help me to take this step are.....

### 8. What would be the signs of success?

I would know I had been successful in taking this step when.....

# Step seventeen:

# Leaders change mindsets

Changing the people is hard enough, but getting people to change how they think is a real challenge. In the past most change in organisations was structural and was less concerned with changing mindsets and more concerned with changing what people did and how they interacted. In today's fast paced, increasingly complex world the major challenge for leaders is changing mindsets or changing how people see the world, how they think about what they do and how they decide what to do. Large scale change requires a shift in perspective, not just a change in priorities. Changing how people think about their work, how they feel about it and changing what they do are the foundations of transformational change.

## What this step means

Changing how people think is more critical than trying to change how they feel or what they do. In fact changing beliefs is the first step in changing behaviour and feelings. Transformational change occurs when people change the way they think about their work and themselves. The biggest gains in organisational performance will come from tapping the potential of the workforce at all levels throughout the organisation. It is a person's mindset that is the greatest limiting factor in human achievement. It is generally more a lack of belief in ability than any lack of ability which is the real issue. Unlocking the potential of people comes from changing the beliefs of individuals about what they can contribute and what they can achieve.

## How this step has changed

Management was primarily concerned with task. Leadership is primarily concerned with people. This is a simple and classical way of differentiating the two, but what it does highlight is that leaders believe that the task is achieved through the talent and contribution of the people being led and thus the major focus is on getting the people right. This means that leaders invest large amounts of time and energy on people, their development and their involvement. It also means that leaders must understand what "makes people tick", their emotions, their motivation, their thinking and their beliefs.

It is the mindsets of the people in the team that are important. Leaders need to understand whether current mindsets are helpful and support the achievement of goals or whether they are counter productive and undermine personal and team achievement. Learning how to change mindsets is an art and a skill and is a personal investment that a leader makes in the development of each individual.

## What this step means for you

As a leader you have to be effective at influencing, educating and inspiring others. It means that you have first to understand your own mindset, including your beliefs and assumptions and appreciate how they influence the world you see. You need also to gain insight into the mindset that others bring to their work. It means that you have to appreciate whether or not beliefs are based upon evidence and some shared objective reality or whether they are primarily subjective and ego driven.

It also means that as a leader you have to find ways to explain difficult concepts and ways to build understanding and agreement. This requires leaders to be skilled at helping people to see things from different perspectives and to be sensitive to the concerns and anxieties that make it difficult for people to embrace new ideas. It means that leaders have to be thoughtful and considerate but in the end also persuasive. Building positive constructive mindsets and helping people to let go of old outmoded ways of thinking are essential tools of leaders today.

## What you can do:

1. Adopt self-reflection

   Set aside a regular time to reflect on your own thinking and consider how open you are to seeing things from different perspectives. How often do you think the same, decide the same and respond the same?

2. Monitor your mindset

   Review some of the decisions you have made and priorities you have set and reflect on how your mindset at the time has influenced these. Is your mindset one from the past or does it reflect the changing world?

3. Develop a deeper understanding of how people think

When discussing issues with people ask them not only what they think but also why they think it. Understanding the "what and the why" is the first step to building influence.

4. Bring new perspectives to the discussion

Gather evidence and research that will challenge the way people think. Keep people informed about the world and the issues we face.

5. Introduce new perspectives

Challenge people to see things from different perspectives. Thinking like a customer, or an investor, or a regulator, or a supplier forces people to see things from different perspectives and can be a powerful tool in changing mindsets.

## A final reminder

Having insight into human psychology is one of the big challenges that leaders face today. The second big challenge is knowing how to influence thinking and to change mindsets. It is the mindset that we have that determines what we see in the world, how we make sense of it and how we determine what is possible. It is our mindset rather than the company strategy that determines what we do and what we don't do. In this way our mindset can be an asset or an anchor. It can help us to see possibilities and to take effective action, or it can blind us to possibility and rob us of opportunity.

As a leader start with your own mindset and gain understanding into how it influences what you see, what you consider and what you do. Use this as a basis for gaining insight into the impact of mindset on others and for developing techniques and expertise for mindset change. The big changes in teams and organisations don't come from structural change they come from mindset change.

## Development plan for mastering this step: Changing Mindsets

### 1.  What more do I need to know?
To take this step I need to know more about.....

### 2. What are the benefits of taking this step?
If I could master this step it would enable me to.....

### 3. What might make this hard to do?
The challenges I face in taking this step are.....

### 4. What would I have to change?
The behaviours I need to adopt to complete this step are.....

## 5. What might be some obstacles?

The things that might stop me from taking this step are.....

## 6. Where do I start?

The first thing I need to do to get started is to.....

## 7. What would help me to succeed?

The supports I would need to put in place to help me to take this step are.....

## 8. What would be the signs of success?

I would know I had been successful in taking this step when.....

# Step eighteen:

# Leaders unlock the hidden value in people and teams

One major difference between managers and leaders is that managers see people as they are and leaders see them as they might be. Leadership is concerned with showing people what they might be and challenging them to be the best they can be. The greatest opportunity for organisations today is the so far unrealised potential of the people within. It is not about getting more people, the competitive advantage lies in getting more from the people that you have. If we accept that through our lives we are all a work in progress, then the work of the leader is to stimulate that progress, to accelerate it and to then harvest the results. Bringing out the hidden value in people and teams is the real work of leaders today.

## What this step means

Leaders are concerned with getting the best out of people with developing talent and unlocking potential. Leaders, because they focus on the future, and because they are motivated by looking for growth, are adept at seeing the potential in people, at finding opportunities for them, and matching the individual to the opportunities. Astute leaders can see the early indicators of success, and because they pay such close attention to the performance and development of people can identify growth pathways early, and change direction quickly if necessary. Everyone has more potential than they exhibit at any time and in any situation. In this way we are all works in progress. The next leap in productivity for organisations will come from finding ways to develop this potential and to tap into this hidden value. It is not what we are, but becoming what we might be that is the great opportunity for the future. Leaders who can unlock this potential and remove the impediments to growth will be in high demand.

## How this step has changed

Once work was about doing your job. Now because the world is changing rapidly, the workplace is also undergoing significant change. Work is increasingly more than a job. It is something which brings meaning and fulfilment to our lives. It is something we embrace, not something we endure. In this environment people also need to change, to learn and to relate in different ways. It is not what people bring to the workplace that is the new competitive advantage. It is what they have the potential to do, and the potential to contribute that organisations seek to tap into.

This issue was highlighted in the book, "Hidden Value: how great companies achieve extraordinary results with ordinary people" by Charles O'Reilly and Jeffrey Pfeffer. Published in 2000 they showed how the best companies sustain their competitive advantage by a set of disciplined processes which bring out the best in the people employed. Growth and long term success comes from unlocking this hidden value. The real opportunity for companies lies in releasing what for so many, and for so much of their careers, remains as hidden potential.

## What this step means for you

It means that as a leader you have to have a genuine desire to develop the potential of the people that you lead. In the first instance it means that you have to believe that all people have greater potential than they display. Exceptional leaders when they recruit people pay as much attention to what they might be, as to what they are now. It means showing an interest in people, their dreams and their beliefs and seeking to understand what really "makes them tick". It means that as a leader you must have a commitment to your own development and the development of others. It is more about psychology than it is about management. As expectations increase and standards rise leaders need the expertise to accelerate human development.

## What you can do:

1. Reflect how passion unlocks potential

   Reflect on how passionate you are about being the best you can be and the extent to which you pass this passion on to others. Do you believe that the people in your team have the potential to do more and do you give them the opportunity, and the room, to grow?

2. Review steps in your own development

   Think about the chapters in your career to date. Write down what motivated you to progress and what you learned from each chapter that helped you to move on to the next.

3. Aim to extract the hidden value

   Consider what you believe to be the next step for each

member of your team. Think about ways you can challenge them and create opportunities either by expanding their jobs or changing their jobs or building their self-belief.

4.  Remove the barriers to self-development

    Take the time to get to know people well and understand what they are motivated to do and what stops them from being the best they can be. Are the barriers more structural, more interpersonal or more personal?

5.  Put in place required support

    Consider what support each individual would need in order to have the confidence to change and the courage to challenge themselves and others.

## A final reminder

All of us are in some way works in progress. Some of us make progress, some of us stall or plateau in our development. Finding ways and means to trigger growth and to kick start learning is what inspiring leaders seek to do. The good news is that today there is greater opportunity available in organisations and greater scope for personal achievement than at any time in history. In fact organisations have to be geared to attracting talent, tapping potential and providing opportunities for growth.

Rapid change, greatly increased competition and escalating expectations, all mean that the game has changed and the stakes are higher. The consequences of success or failure are clearer and the reality comes faster. We could once just respond by improving human performance. Now the only sustainable response is to do that and at the same time create future opportunities. It is not being better with what we have now that is the key, it is being better at what we might be.

## Development plan for mastering this step: Unlocking the Hidden Value in People and Teams

### 1. What more do I need to know?

To take this step I need to know more about.....

### 2. What are the benefits of taking this step?

If I could master this step it would enable me to.....

### 3. What might make this hard to do?

The challenges I face in taking this step are.....

### 4. What would I have to change?

The behaviours I need to adopt to complete this step are.....

## 5. What might be some obstacles?

The things that might stop me from taking this step are.....

## 6. Where do I start?

The first thing I need to do to get started is to.....

## 7. What would help me to succeed?

The supports I would need to put in place to help me to take this step are.....

## 8. What would be the signs of success?

I would know I had been successful in taking this step when.....

# Step nineteen:

# Leaders embrace learning and drive change

The only antidote to change is our ability to learn. All human progress relies on our ability to learn and to adapt. In a very real way long term sustainable achievement, depends on our ability to continually learn faster than the rate of change we are experiencing. Pro-active change or being ahead of the game is the preferred mode for industry leaders. In a highly competitive environment reactive change or being a fast follower is also required. Leaders must build a culture that embraces learning and must model behaviours that promote change. Leaders must be the chief advocates for change and through their behaviour model what this change looks like. In a world of constant change life-long learning is essential.

**What this step means**

Leaders today must be passionate about learning. They also must embrace change and demonstrate that learning is the only effective response to change. Getting the balance between learning and change right is a challenge for leaders. A rate of change significantly greater than a person's capacity to learn leads to burnout and stress. A capacity to learn significantly greater than the degree of change leads to frustration and boredom. Many leaders accept new challenges because they enjoy the thrill of a steep learning curve. They create a learning environment for themselves and a learning culture for the people they lead.

Leaders are restless, passionate and constantly challenging the status quo. They are curious and open minded and constantly looking to find a better way forward. They understand that the future will not be more of the same and that it is our ability to adapt and to learn quickly which will determine our success on the journey. Leaders today don't think of change management as an additional assignment or a special challenge. They appreciate that managing change is a core ingredient of leadership. You cannot have leadership without a desire for change.

**How this step has changed**

For a long time managers were required to put a priority on consistency over adaptability. The manager's job was to find that which didn't change and to lock standard operating procedures into place.  A rapidly changing global environment, and escalating competitive pressures, means that organisations have to find ways to change and to harness more of the brainpower and imagination of the entire workforce. No longer is one brain sufficient. The boss no matter how bright cannot supply all of the answers in an increasingly complex world.

 In the early 1990's Peter Senge's book, The Fifth Discipline, generated great interest in the concept of the learning organisation. His central proposition was that the only sustainable competitive advantage was an organisation's ability to learn and to turn its learning quickly into practice. It replaced the old idea that change was an event, with the idea that change was really a process of continual learning. It put forward the proposition that effective learning organisations were able to bring bright people together to build processes and systems which embedded a learning discipline into the way things were done. Today the ability to learn from experience, to share this learning and to be able to build it into change across an organisation is considered an essential driver of long term strategic success.

## What this step means for you

It means an acceptance that the capabilities you have today will not be the ones required by you tomorrow, and that the insights you have today will not be those that will guide thinking in the future. It means that you will need to be curious, open to new ways of doing things and prepared to change even the things that are an established part of your repertoire. It means accepting the notion that today's core strengths may be limiting factors in the future. It means understanding that the things that drive success early in a career, such as personal mastery, will not be the same as those that drive executive success later in a career, such as the ability to get results through others. Never being satisfied and having an on-going commitment to self improvement and to development will be two key indicators of effective future leadership.

The only evidence of learning is change in behaviour. You can read a book about riding a bike but this does not guarantee that you can ride. The only proof that you have learnt how to ride is demonstrated performance on a bicycle. This is the difference between learning and knowledge. Knowledge is knowing how to do something, learning is showing you can do it. The best leaders turn theory into practice and understand that changed behaviour is an indicator of how much they have learnt. As a leader, if the world doesn't change, then you will not need to learn a great deal. However, the greater the challenge faced, and the faster the pace of change, the more behaviour must change and the greater the learning must be.

**What you can do:**

1.  Assess your preferred learning style

    Reflect on your own learning style and how you best learn and the extent to which you use this learning style effectively for your own personal growth and development.

2.  Review past challenges and learning

    Think about major challenges you have faced in a personal or professional sense. What did you do, what did you learn, what would you change next time?

3.  Make learning a priority

    The evidence of learning is change in behaviour, so the more we need to learn the more we need to change our behaviour. Take the time to have a regular review of the challenges you face and how you are responding, and the extent to which you are actively learning.

4.  Assess future challenges and learning

    Identify future challenges that you will most likely face and discuss with mentors a learning program now to prepare you to deal with them.

5.  Make room for new learning

    Review some of the behaviours or activities that you should let go of now so that you can make room for the new.

## A final reminder

Learning and change go together. If you believe that the world will be different in the future then you must embrace change. If you believe that the challenges you will face and the skills you will need will be different then you have to embrace learning. The greatest dangers for leaders today are complacency and arrogance. That is, believing that they have no need to learn and believing that they have nothing left to learn. Leadership requires challenging the status quo and embracing new ways of thinking and doing things. When a leader feels that he/she is in a comfort zone, then that may be an early warning that that leader has plateaued. How do you know if you are in a comfort zone? By definition, it is when you are feeling comfortable and experience no discomfort. If you never feel challenged and never feel out of your depth, then be aware because you may also have shut down your learning.

## Development plan for mastering this step: Embracing learning, driving change

**1.  What more do I need to know?**

To take this step I need to know more about.....

**2. What are the benefits of taking this step?**

If I could master this step it would enable me to.....

**3. What might make this hard to do?**

The challenges I face in taking this step are.....

**4. What would I have to change?**

The behaviours I need to adopt to complete this step are.....

### 5. What might be some obstacles?

The things that might stop me from taking this step are.....

### 6. Where do I start?

The first thing I need to do to get started is to.....

### 7. What would help me to succeed?

The supports I would need to put in place to help me to take this step are.....

### 8. What would be the signs of success?

I would know I had been successful in taking this step when.....

# Step twenty:

# Leaders set a positive example

Leaders are always on display and people take notice of how their leaders behave at work and also when they are not at work. They notice whether what they say is different on formal, or informal, occasions. People want to assess if what leaders say is what they genuinely believe. They observe their behaviour and make judgements about the values they hold. In order to have this level of personal authenticity leaders need a close alignment between what they say and what they believe. They also need a high level of emotional intelligence. They need to be aware of their own feelings and mood and manage these and be aware of how these affect the mood of the people they lead.

Terry Lee

## What this step means

Leaders must be careful of the example they set and the behaviour they display. People are always watching to see whether the people who lead them are genuine or not. It is from their behaviour that leaders develop a reputation and it is this reputation that influences how people react and relate to them. The problem is when the leader's reputation is not consistent with the leader's intent or with his/her own self-assessment. When who I think I am is not how people see me then I have a credibility problem. Credibility is built when the leader's identity is expressed through their behaviour. Thus leaders knowing what they stand for and then ensuring that this is what people see are the leaders who are seen as authentic. A reputation once established is very hard to shift and so it is important for leaders to carefully monitor the reputation that they are building. People today are looking for leaders, as always, who achieve results but they are especially looking for those who achieve results through people.

## How this step has changed

Leaders are expected to be a great deal more sophisticated today. In the past people were not really surprised if their leaders behaved badly or inappropriately. It would not be unusual for command and control leaders to be autocrats, and there would be little surprise even if they were abusive or condescending. Temper tantrums and other displays of negative emotion were widely tolerated as just part of what goes with the person. We would think today that these leaders had little self control and they would lose a great deal of respect from colleagues. We also know these behaviours undermine trust and openness and are likely to build cultures of cynicism and underperformance.

## What this step means for you

Just as self awareness is critical for leaders, so too is self management. Leaders today need the discipline to behave not only with dignity but also in accordance with the values they are trying to promote. As a leader you cannot just do what you want to do, you have to do what is required of you as a leader. This means being aware of your impact on the team at all times and choosing carefully what you say and do. Leaders need the ability to restrain impulses that are not helpful and to take actions which are not only useful today but are effective in supporting the long term strategy. Having the discipline to self manage, to monitor one's impact, and to live according to one's principles are important leadership disciplines.

**What you can do:**

1.  Building your reputation

    Reflect upon the reputation you have in your personal and professional life. Is this the reputation that that you want and is it consistent with your self-perception? Is based on the principles and values that are truly important to you?

2.  Decide important behavioural attributes

    Write down the behaviours that you would like to think are a fundamental part of your reputation. Reflect on your identity as a leader and list the behaviours that are personally not acceptable to you and you would not like to be associated with. Consider whether some behaviours are inconsistent with who you think you really are.

3.  Be a centre of influence

    Who looks up to you and is influenced by you, and looks to you for guidance as to what to do and what not to do? Are you proud of the role model you are? Do you go out of your way to build connections with a wide range of people?

4.  See yourself in action

    Observe a video of yourself in meetings so you can become more aware of your typical behaviours. When you see yourself in action whether this person would inspire you.

5.  Assess your impact

    Watch the reactions that others have to what you do. Try some new behaviours in meetings to see what happens. Do you hold yourself to the same standards that you expect of others?

## A final reminder

We all have an impact on others. The challenge for leaders is knowing whether the impact is good or bad, and whether it is the impact intended. Just doing what you want to do is self-indulgent. Leadership is not about ego and what makes me feel important it is about impact on the lives of others. All leaders have a responsibility to develop people and to help them to succeed. They also have a responsibility to the organisations and communities that they serve. This means that must be disciplined in what they do and deliberate in how they behave. They should also be aware that their impact forms the basis of their reputation and that in turn determines the opportunities that are presented to them.

## Development plan for mastering this step: Setting a positive example

**1.  What more do I need to know?**

To take this step I need to know more about.....

**2. What are the benefits of taking this step?**

If I could master this step it would enable me to.....

**3. What might make this hard to do?**

The challenges I face in taking this step are.....

**4. What would I have to change?**

The behaviours I need to adopt to complete this step are.....

### 5. What might be some obstacles?

The things that might stop me from taking this step are.....

### 6. Where do I start?

The first thing I need to do to get started is to.....

### 7. What would help me to succeed?

The supports I would need to put in place to help me to take this step are.....

### 8. What would be the signs of success?

I would know I had been successful in taking this step when.....

# Step twenty-one:

# Leaders have a clear strategic agenda

Leaders have focus and a clearly defined strategic agenda. This enables them to define goals and key priorities and this means that they can put their energies where they will deliver most value. Energy follows focus and if the leader is trying to do everything then his/her energy will be everywhere. In this situation we say that the leader's efforts are spread thin and nothing gets done really well. A leader with a clear focus can direct energy to where there is the greatest strategic advantage to be gained. Leaders don't have to do everything. In fact those who try to do it all, leave little room for their people to grow. Creating an environment where people can step up, and step forward, to receive a new challenge is the real skill of the artful leader.

## What this step means

Leaders don't do things by accident, by default or by luck. Of course there is an element of all three in a complex and rapidly changing world. It may be that it is the leader's intuition rather than any certainty that comes into play, but it is probably intuition honed by experience and reflection on that experience. It is an emotional competency of leadership, where the leader "knows" when something just "feels right". Leaders have an agenda and are clear about the difference that they want to make and this can be seen in their strategic focus and in their clearly defined priorities. Leaders are not impulsive but they certainly can be spontaneous. They have to be decisive, and often decisive without all of the information required to make a decision with absolute certainty. Taking considered risks is an essential attribute of exceptional leaders.

Leadership takes courage and confidence. Leaders are prepared to step forward and to challenge the ways things are done because they have belief in the future. Whilst they might look to the past for lessons, they look to the future for inspiration. Leaders are not prepared to sit still. Waiting for someone else to act is not leadership. Leaders have a commitment to the future and to finding a better way to do things. They are compelled to act.

## How this step has changed

Whilst managers were more likely to be "minding the store" leaders were more likely to be changing it or improving it. Leaders are not custodians of the status quo, they come with a clear agenda and with a specific intent to achieve something worthwhile. They are motivated by a deeper sense of purpose and attracted by the challenge of change. Leaders seek opportunities where they can test themselves and prove themselves and where they can support others to achieve success. When they take a new assignment, their specific objective may not be clear, nor their strategic direction certain. Leaders take the time to listen and learn and to observe and assess. Once they have made their judgement they lay out a path forward and invite others to join in the journey. Having a clear agenda enables leaders to have a clear focus and set clear priorities and to remove distractions. It enables them to concentrate on the main event.

## What this step means for you

It means be certain about why you work and why you accept challenges. It means that you must be confident about what you bring to any situation and the basic principles that you will deploy to achieve shared vision. It means that before you accept assignments you need to reflect on what you believe you bring and what resources you will need to be successful. The best leaders today are driven by vision and are compelled by purpose. It means that whatever you do be present in the moment and be a full participant, not just a casual observer. It means that if you accept a challenge, fully commit to it, but have enough of you a little removed to keep things in perspective.

Being immersed in a challenge is where leaders get their passion. Being overwhelmed by the challenge does not enable the leader to see the strategic context and to make short term decisions in the light of the long term objectives. Leaders can become so passionate about a cause that they become over zealous and in the process lose objectivity and the ability to see different solutions. Keeping an open mind and being prepared to change perspective, and at the same time being passionately committed to a cause, is a balance that leaders need to strike every day.

## What you can do:

1. Bring clarity and focus to your work and your life

   Reflect on the extent to which you bring a definite strategic agenda to what you do and the extent to which you can maintain focus even in the midst of distraction?

2. Write a statement of purpose

   Craft a statement of leadership purpose which defines what you have come to do and the principles that will guide the way you act.

3. Share your leadership purpose

   Share with people and teams around you your purpose, your passions and your priorities.

4. Develop a strategic mindset

   Keep up to speed with industry shifts and changes in the strategic environment. Study how organisations build capabilities that give them a competitive advantage. Develop a deep understanding of how competitive advantage is changing in your industry and globally.

5. Cultivate a strategic network

   Mix with people who are passionate about strategic thinking and build a network of people you can bounce ideas off and who will challenge your thinking.

**A final reminder**

If you don't want to change the world in some way, then you probably shouldn't aspire to be a leader. Being an impediment to human progress is not a noble calling and stifling human initiative is not doing others a favour. It doesn't mean the change has to be earth shattering. You don't have to be a megalomaniac to want to improve the human condition. It can simply mean that you want to play your role in human progress and that you simply want to enhance the development of the people you lead. For real leaders at their core is the motivation to make a difference. You decide the difference that you want to make. Helping people to change and helping to change things for the better is not only worthwhile, but is a contribution you make to the communities you serve. The worst thing that you can do is to stand in the way and block progress. The starting point is to decide what you stand for and to decide what sort of leader you want to be, and more importantly what sort of leader your people need you to be.

## Development plan for mastering this step: Having a Clear Strategic Agenda

1. **What more do I need to know?**

   To take this step I need to know more about.....

2. **What are the benefits of taking this step?**

   If I could master this step it would enable me to.....

3. **What might make this hard to do?**

   The challenges I face in taking this step are.....

4. **What would I have to change?**

   The behaviours I need to adopt to complete this step are.....

## 5. What might be some obstacles?
The things that might stop me from taking this step are.....

## 6. Where do I start?
The first thing I need to do to get started is to.....

## 7. What would help me to succeed?
The supports I would need to put in place to help me to take this step are.....

## 8. What would be the signs of success?
I would know I had been successful in taking this step when.....

# Conclusion

**And so what does this all mean for you?**

Be the leader you yearn to be and that your people need you to be. Don't be a leader by default or by accident. Certainly circumstance can help, but make sure that you put yourself in the best position to deal effectively with the circumstances you find yourself in. The best approach of all is to seek the circumstances that will enable you to have your best chance of success and make the maximum contribution to the people you lead.

Leaders today must be equally comfortable working with feelings and emotions as working with ideas and concepts. Understanding the mood of a team is a prerequisite for influencing the team and for helping people to move forward. The mood will colour perceptions and determine how a message is received. Mood also provides energy, both positive and negative. Effective leadership means identifying the mood, assessing the impact of the mood and finding ways to influence the mood so that it is most productive.

If people are in a bad mood there is no point in trying to be upbeat or trying to cheer them up. If they are cynical it would be foolish to assume that a positive message will be received at face value. The leader must accept the mood, help the team to move through it, and then with caring team building and open communication build the mood that will be most productive and conducive to success. It doesn't mean denying moods. It means dealing with them as they are and then helping people to move on. Building a mindset that is positive and constructive and opportunity focused is an empowering leadership act.

All people in their work deserve and are entitled to excellent leadership. There is no one who has a greater impact on the quality of your life at work than the person you report to. Leaders can enrich the experience at work by their genuine care and belief in the ability of all people to grow and to perform, or they can diminish that experience through limiting the opportunities available to people. Exceptional leaders get exceptional results over time. The results required will guide leaders in the impact they need to have. The urgency for change will determine the timeline given. Getting the best out of people and helping them to be successful even beyond their own expectations is the legacy of exceptional leadership.

Leaders are always in demand. As demands on organisation increase, and increase from a diverse range of stakeholders, then expectations of leaders also rise. It is the calibre of leaders and having sufficient of them that is a pre-requisite for organisational success. In many ways the greatest impediment to success is having enough leaders to lead it. It is leadership that is so often the greatest determinant of success or failure. Insufficient leaders will put a hand brake on growth, and growing too quickly beyond your capacity to provide leadership at all levels can be a serious risk.

Leadership is a core capability of excellent organisations. Everyone can show leadership when they use their initiative to help the team to succeed. Leaving leadership to leaders robs an organisation of considerable leadership potential and responsibility. Whilst people in formal leadership roles have a responsibility to display leadership, they must also make sure that they do not remove the opportunity for others to show leadership. Using your initiative to help the team to win and going out of your way to execute the strategy are leadership acts that can be exhibited by anyone, anywhere and at anytime.

So finally, exceptional leaders renew themselves. This is what makes them exceptional over time. They invest in themselves. They invest time and energy in their own development and are constantly searching for ways to improve. Exceptional leaders have carefully prepared, personal development plans for themselves, which provide pathways to their goals. The best also have networks of mentors who can help them with specific areas of understanding and skill development. No longer is one mentor sufficient. In a complex world where much is demanded, you need a range of mentors who can satisfy different needs. Leaders need mentors who can support their technical development, their personal development, and their strategic development.

Most of all you need a network of mentors who can help you to fulfil your true potential as a leader. All of us need mentors, people who care about us and challenge us and support us on our journey. These are people who will be honest and direct when necessary and supportive and reassuring at other times. They are people who are prepared to help us to grow as individuals and they do so not only because they care, but also because their contribution is appreciated. Finding mentors and nurturing the relationship is an important growth factor. Being a mentor for others yourself is an important leadership contribution.

The faster the world changes and the greater the challenges we face as individuals and organisations, the more leadership we need. If there is no change, no leadership is required. In the complex world we live in today, we need exceptional leadership at the individual and collective level. We need individuals who will assume personal leadership for their own lives. We need team leaders who will enrich and develop the teams they lead. We need strategic leaders who will build organisations that are good for people, good for business and good for the planet.

Today more than ever, we need strong leadership capability at all levels in our institutions. We need this leadership widely dispersed throughout our teams and deeply embedded within individuals who are stepping up to accept the real challenges we face today. The leadership opportunity today is like never before. Never before has there been such an opportunity to truly lead and never before has there been a greater need for such broadly based leadership.

How well we meet these challenges as people, as teams and as organisations will be up to us. Whether or not we seize this opportunity will depend upon the extent to which we are prepared to step up to lead, not simply step away.

And the curious possibility is that the final step in this broad transformation of leadership may not be simply stepping up to leadership, but more properly stepping into leadership. Being the leader you truly are in a way that is uniquely yours. The promise of leadership may be bringing more of who you truly are to the art of leadership, but then refining that with the skills and capabilities developed through the science of leadership.

# About the Author

Terry lives in Melbourne, Australia, and is a leadership psychologist who brings the insights of psychology to the practice of management. He works primarily with leaders and leadership teams wanting to step up to the leadership required to unlock the potential of the people and teams that they lead. He has considerable experience working across industries, and across geographies, in transformational change, culture design and the development of authentic leaders at all levels who bring purpose, passion and principles to their practice of leadership.

Terry was previously Head of Leadership at Mt. Eliza Business School in Melbourne, where he also designed and directed the Advanced Management Program which is the school's premier leadership program. Today he works globally with values driven companies and has long term relationships with clients such as Wesfarmers, Bunnings Warehouse, Officeworks, Cisco Systems, Fuji Xerox, Honda, and Clayton Utz Lawyers.

Terry's leadership purpose is "to inspire managers to transform the lives of the people they lead."

He can be reached at www.leadership.com.au

www.ingramcontent.com/pod-product-compliance
Lightning Source LLC
Chambersburg PA
CBHW021058210326
41598CB00016B/1255